Tales from

You Wouldn't do it for the Money !

Sherry Tomlinson

Library of Congress Cataloging-in-Publication Data
ISBN 0-9766230-0-5

Editors: Heidi Utz, John Edmonds
Book Designer: Veronique Meurgues

Photo credits (cover): U.S. Fish and Wildlife Service
Photo of black bear: Mike Bender

Contact info: www.sherrytomlinson.alaskawriters.com
Anchorage, Alaska

Printed in Canada.

Note from the author:
*Names and the details of stories have been fictionalized
to protect the privacy of bed and breakfast guests.*

Contents

Sherry's Recipes

Welcome

Bed-and-breakfast guests are smart and funny, and they teach me lessons about life. For instance, I've learned that the happiest retirees are those who forget what they once did for a living. She's no longer a doctor; she's now a bird-watcher. Once a teacher, he's now a student of Renaissance art. The businessman and his wife are "out to pasture" with a recently purchased horse ranch. New lives. Smart.

And funny. Two warm, outgoing British women staying with us were definitely a couple. When one of them picked up Gracie, our old housecat, I tried to explain: "She's really a he, but we realized it only when an elderly neighbor complained. Gracie was going through the neighbor's cat door, into the house, and harassing a harem of female cats. We were shocked when we turned Gracie upside down. Upon closer inspection, we still didn't see anything significant enough to call Gracie a boy. So the name stuck."

Picking Gracie up, my guest counseled him/her: "Look, Gracie, you don't have to take this, you know. There's help out there for the sexually confused. Stand up for yourself. You can't just hang out in the closet!"

Five sisters taught me a lesson about growing older. They were here for a few days to honor the eldest sister's hundredth birthday. Not one of them was younger than eighty, but they were all stylish. No baggy clothes for these ladies. Two of my guests who used walkers looked elegant in their fashionable pantsuits. Their fingers were arthritic but well manicured. When the women sat down to breakfast, their makeup was perfect. They smelled like expensive French perfume.

What did they talk about? Family gossip, books they were reading, the price of eggs in 1945. They never discussed what body part was hurting today. Even though I knew they must be experiencing the aches and pains of age, I never heard one of them complain.

If my back hurts in the morning or my leg feels gimpy, I think of the ladies and try to suck it up. If five beautiful old women can have courage, so can I.

Every guest brings life to this home. One memorable couple from New York arrived late in the afternoon wound tighter than the watches on their wrists. I've never been to New York, but I have a sort of Woody Allen image of beautiful, complex people who wear black and are always in a hurry. The couple's presence brought a nervous, cell-phone-ringing, fast-talking intensity to the house, as out of place as my "What, me worry?" attitude might be in Manhattan.

The couple had booked a ten-day tour with an Alaska wilderness outfitter. I thought: "Boy, these folks will go nuts. Workaholics last about three days before they need an adrenalin rush. Bet they'll be back within five."

Ten days later, the New Yorkers returned. They'd stayed in cabins at the end of the road in Denali National Park and used an outhouse for the first time. They ate a fish they themselves caught in the Yukon River and were now proudly wearing new flannel shirts. They looked like Alaskans.

Incredibly, they got to see The Mountain. When Denali threw off her cloudy veil for a rare appearance, their guide told them to put away their cameras. He gave each of the guests a glass of plum wine and urged them to "go find a place to be by yourself, enjoy your wine as you look at the mountain, and search for inner peace."

The mountain, the wine, and the private moment must have worked, because my guests looked radiant. On their last night, as the tour group sat around the campfire, their guide gave each of them an envelope. Inside the envelope was an informational sheet about an Alaska animal. That animal was to become their new totemic identity.

"I am Otter," said my female guest. "I swim with the flow of the waters of life. I am playful and sleek and adaptable. I am Otter."

"And I am Bear," offered her husband. "I have physical strength and canny intelligence. I fish the waters, eat off the land. I find what I need. I am Bear."

They were transformed. I don't know how long the totemic spirits stayed with them once they returned home, but it was a treat to see my guests take a break in their life. After they left, I sent the wilderness outfitters the only fan letter I've ever written.

At the end of that summer, after almost twenty years of running a bed-and-breakfast in Alaska, I commented to my husband: "This was the greatest year we've ever had. Are we getting better? Was it us or the guests?"

My husband answered without hesitation: "The guests. Absolutely."

From wilderness adventurers to artists and architects, families with children to sweet retirees, guests are fun to be with. I do believe that when they go home fresh from their Alaska adventures, they'll tell stories about the mountains and the animals. They'll show more pictures than their friends and families could possibly act interested in. They'll talk about the food they ate. But the most animated stories they tell will be about the people they've met.

CHAPTER 1

Neighborhood Watch

"I had a wonderful stay. Sorry about all the confusion last night."

—bed and breakfast guest—

When summer comes to Alaska, it's like waking from a long dream. Winter is shucked to the back of the closet like a heavy coat. By the solstice, in June, the neighborhood has a street-party atmosphere. At ten o'clock at night there are skateboards, bikes and trikes, and an ice cream truck with "It's a Small World" on replay. There's the whack-whack of tennis balls, and car doors slam as little-leaguers climb into the back seat of an SUV. A dog barks.

In the play park across the street from our house, children ride red plastic broncos and screech when they're shot with a water pistol. It's summer in Alaska. Party time!

I hear a tired mother yell to her youngster, "Get in here

and get to bed!"

"But, Mom, we were just getting up a Frisbee game."

"I don't care. TIME FOR BED!"

"But, Mom, I won't be able to sleep. Dad's still mowing the lawn."

Alaska nights are tough on parents.

My husband and I are sitting on the front patio talking with friends when a taxi drives up with two of our evening's bed and breakfast guests. After unloading passengers and luggage, the taxi driver backs out of the driveway very slowly. There are kids, dogs, and bikes to dodge.

The couple turns to look across the lawn toward the park. There is a path across a green expanse and a view of Cook Inlet beyond. The sky is just starting to pink up as the sun makes a good-night curtsey.

"Will it get dark tonight?" asks our guest.

"No, it won't. The sun will do a little dip behind the trees, the night will turn dusky, and by 2:00 a.m. or so, it starts to turn light again."

"Why don't you join us after we put up your luggage?" I ask. "Would you like a glass of wine? Tea?"

Our guests may have been on a plane sitting through multiple time zones. They relax as they fold into lawn chairs. As they breathe in the cool, clean-smelling air of an Alaska night, you can see it in their faces. They're hooked.

We'll take our guests to a warm, comfortable room, later, but right now we'll watch the kid-biker-skater-jogger-walker show go by while we tell a few jokes, sip our wine, get acquainted, and, well, just chitchat.

I've been "enjoying the moment" with guests since 1986, when I opened the bed and breakfast in a cute house I called my "bungaloid." Originally a small tract house, it has since been expanded, remodeled, and landscaped right up to the lot lines. There's also a greenhouse, a shed, a gazebo, and a pond for the fish. Wherever there has been an open space, I've planted a garden. "Loved your Japanese-English garden," wrote one guest.

The house is blue with wraparound fences and a long green lawn with an wild mock-orange bush that, when in bloom, flings its fragrance into the air like a bridal bouquet. I think the place looks like home.

I wasn't so confident in the beginning. A bed and

3

breakfast business in this neighborhood was something new. Though it was legal to have one, I cared what my neighbors thought in this old, established neighborhood.

As neighbors, we had a high tolerance for each other's hobbies. If one of us kept some rabbits or birds or put up an extra utility shed, no one cared. We watched out for each other, fed each other's pets, watered plants, offered an ear, a shoulder, and a cup of coffee to help get through life's dramas.

Still, people were curious. They asked me about the new bed and breakfast enterprise. Would there be a lot more traffic? What about parking? Noise? Was it safe for a woman to have people in her house? What about men on their own? Did I have a lock on my bedroom door? Though my neighbors were also my friends, I was a little nervous. I felt I was being watched, by nice people with high standards.

One of my first guests was a trekker from a southern state. He would be spending a month in the Alaska Range, learning wilderness skills. When the cab dropped him and his backpack in the driveway, I shook hands with a soft-eyed youngster. In a slow Southern drawl, he thanked me for letting him stay. As he hefted his bag over his shoulder, he gallantly opened the front door for me. He was easily over six feet tall, and shy. He was seventeen years old, he'd never been away from home, and he was about to spend a month in the wilderness.

I asked my young guest, "How was your flight up? Did you see the mountains?"

"Yes, ma'am, I did." He answered.

"What'd you think of them? Pretty spectacular, huh?

"Yes, but I'm feeling a bit overwhelmed right now," he said. "We flew for hours and didn't see anything but sky, water, and mountaintops. I've hiked in the Appalachians, but I've never seen mountains that big. It took my breath away!"

I thought he looked a little pale. He'll be all right, I thought. Send him on a long walk so he'll be tired enough to sleep tonight.

"We're one mile from a great shopping mall," I told him. "It has a café, a bookstore with an espresso bar, and an outdoor clothing outlet. Got all the gear you need for the

5

course? Have you eaten? It's a great place for a snack."

"I don't think I could eat right now. I've got the jitters so bad, Ma'am," he replied. "But I'd like to take a walk and check out the store."

Soon my guest headed out, map in hand, out of sight and out of mind for the next few hours.

While my trekker was gone, I welcomed a pleasant fiftyish couple from Georgia, Mr. and Mrs. Wilson. They would be joining a cruise from Seward, Alaska, to Vancouver, British-Columbia. They were here for a few days to take a look around Anchorage. Exhausted from the long flight to Alaska, they were looking forward to a relaxing night in our home.

With Mr. and Mrs. Wilson settled in and my young trekker off on his own, I thought: "Hey, I could go out for the evening. Free at last." After sushi, sake, and a romantic comedy at the local six-plex, I felt like I'd had a mini-vacation. I headed home, totally oblivious to the fact that when I was at the movies, there had been an unromantic comedy playing to a front row crowd of my neighbors.

I had just settled in on the front patio with a cup of tea

in hand when the Wilsons hurried up the driveway from an evening walk. They had a "while you were away" story. Uh-oh.

"There was a big to-do tonight," explained Mrs. Wilson. "Your young guest sure got into a mess, bless his heart. He's already gone to bed."

Good grief. "What happened?" I asked.

"Well, Mr. Wilson said, "your guest was walking home when a car stopped at the curb. Two gals inside asked if he'd like a ride."

"Seems innocent to me," said Mrs. Wilson. "How was he to know?"

"Honey, the guy is old enough to know a bad business when he sees it," Mr. Wilson said.

"Well, how was he to know the girls were such bad drivers? Goodness!" his wife replied.

Mr. Wilson explained. "They were both stinking drunk and drove real wild all around the parking lot before jumping the parking lot barrier. That's what the policeman said."

"Police?" I thought. Egads.

"Then," Mr. Wilson continued, "the two gals drove

down the hill probably headed for the next bar when they spotted our young friend walking in the same direction. They stopped to offer him a ride.

"He didn't!"

"Yep," he did. "Got into the car."

What was he thinking?

The rest of their story didn't get better. The women gave our guy a fast ride down the street, bounced against a median strip, and raced fast and furious on toward the bed and breakfast. By this time, they had company.

Police cars with their lights and sirens screaming gave plenty of warning for my neighbors to catch the action. By the time the inebriated ladies and my guest pulled into the driveway, noses were pressed against windows.

At this point, the police pulled everyone out of the car. My guest was confused. One of the officers ID'd the ladies as hookers. "We know who these ladies are, mister (jabbing his finger at my guest). That makes you a customer!" barked the officer. "Can I see your ID, please?"

"I, um, don't have it with me right now, sir." Things were going south real fast.

I guess being polite didn't help, because my guest found himself spread-eagled against the car doors. The alcohol infused girls were foul-mouthed, and getting louder. One of them ran away to a neighbor's house screaming obscenities, pounding on their door, and demanding to use the telephone. After another loud argument on my neighbor's front porch, the officer brought the handcuffed girl back to our driveway. Could it get any worse?

Meanwhile, abandoning all pretenses, my neighbor Tom brought out a kitchen chair, propped it up against the house, and sat down with a glass of vino to enjoy the show.

"We heard all the noise," said Mrs. Wilson. We came out to see what was going on. There was your guest under arrest, and those young women were swearing something awful!"

"We talked to the officer," Mr. Wilson said. "We didn't want there to be a problem for you, so we told the officer: 'We're old friends of the family. Our friend had to go to the store, but she'll be back soon. We can vouch for this young man. This is not his car, he wasn't driving, and he is who he says he is. Really.'"

"We didn't say bed and breakfast guests," added Mrs. Wilson. The Wilsons had done a kind thing, God bless 'em. They lied.

Who wouldn't believe this sweet couple? The officers let my trekker go. They arrested both young women and took them away. Everyone went to bed. Tom and the rest of the neighbors disappeared. Peace prevailed.

At breakfast the next morning, my guest was apologetic.

"I'm sorry about all the fuss last night. Hitching a ride is no big deal where I come from. Hope I didn't make a problem for you."

"Hey, it's no big deal. How were you to know? I guess we're getting to be a big city. You all right?"

"Sure," he replied. "You know, I recently became born again into the faith. It's made all the difference in my personality. I used to be socially naive and awkward, but I think I'm getting more confident."

What could I say? Not to worry. Thanks for staying with us. And be careful out in those mountains, OK?

After my guests had checked out, I had time to think about last night's drama over my morning coffee. How was it going to play with the neighbors? Individually, the words "bed and breakfast" and "police and ladies" are fine. Together, they sound disastrous.

Here I'd been worried about parking! I really wanted the business I'd put in my neighbors backyards to be invisible. Last night's scene had enough police action to be on one of those on-the-spot TV shows with the police collaring criminals. It had it all: wild driving, wild women, and possibly their john. That would make me?

I walked outside the front door to get the morning paper, hoping I would not have to make eye contact with anyone I knew.

"Good morning," Tom said, tossing me the newspaper as if nothing had happened. "Another day in paradise, what?"

"Sure is, Tom," I answered. "Nice and peaceful. Like a fresh blueberry scone to go with that coffee you have in your hand?"

"You bet, dearie. Catch you later."

Got friendship, tolerance, and a patio with a view.

Got classy neighbors too.

CHAPTER 2

When Wild Mammals Meet!

"Stomped by moose before, skier unloads with .44"

—Anchorage Daily News headline, March 20, 2004—

"It pinned its ears back, lowered its head and commenced to charge. When the moose was about seven yards away, I shot."

—skier in Anchorage's Kincaid Park—

When guests come to Alaska, they want to see moose. Moose have to be one of the largest and ugliest mammals in North America. Ugly doesn't matter to guests; they still want a photo. To me there's nothing cute about a moose when he's snacking on my daffodils, although I'll admit, an adult bull with a full rack is definitely impressive. To appreciate his size, you need to see one on his hind legs, hairy brown neck stretched up to gather leaves from a willow tree, antlers swaying back and forth as he forages.

Moose can be almost invisible when bedded down in deep snow. We have to warn guests when they take a stroll through the neighborhood that a moose encounter can be bone crunching, even deadly. Several people have been stomped to death the last few years. Victims were skiing, walking between classes at the university, or rescuing a barking dog. Still there is little public enthusiasm for having a urban pet-hunting season in the streets of Anchorage. Most of us love the big, ugly ungulates.

* * *

One summer, two of our guests, Jeff and Debra were to observe a nasty encounter between a moose and a pest of the two-legged variety.

Jeff was a frequent and well-liked guest at the bed and breakfast. A high-energy businessman, he kept his fishing gear in the trunk of rented car just in case a recreational opportunity presented itself. We got along so well, Jeff threatened to have his stuff sent up so he could move in with us.

Jeff clearly missed his young wife. She would soon

join him for a few days. It would be her first trip to Alaska. Jeff wanted Debra to love Alaska as much as he did. He talked about her constantly and was making us all crazy with his antsiness. He was excited about showing his wife his favorite wilderness spots. She would be here one night with us, then off to the Kenai Peninsula for two nights of fishing.

When Debra arrived, she was pretty and lively. It was a soggy night with rain and wind beating against the dining room window. Debra called the gloomy weather "dramatic." Good attitude!

Jeff had a map flattened out on the kitchen table showing Debra where they would go fishing on the Kenai River. He promised her clear streams, mountain majesty, and a cozy cabin for two.

After breakfast the next morning, they left in high spirits. The day, autumn crisp and clear, started off nicely with a beautiful drive around Turnagain Arm. As they neared the Kenai River, they slowed to see why so many cars were parked by the roadside. After stopping to get out of their car, they were astonished to see a gigantic bull moose standing in a nearby meadow.

The moose was a beauty. Fall fat; he was dipping his head into the wet marsh. As he pulled out grassy vegetation and lifted his head, the water streamed over his antlers and down his dark back. His majestic rack would look great in the photos. He was a dramatic crowd pleaser. Everyone was excited, snapping pictures and talking in hushed tones.

The spectators looked up, startled, when a man in a large pickup pulled over to the side of the road, braking hard and spinning gravel. He stepped out of the truck dressed in a red plaid shirt, a hunter's cap, and an arrogant walk. He was everyone's stereotype of a big, bad hunter.

The newcomer eyed the moose, strode back to his truck, got into the cab, and pulled a gun off a rack. It was one of those slow-mo scenes when you can't believe what's happening.

As he approached the edge of the meadow, he raised his rifle to take aim. Onlookers protested: "What are you doing? You can't shoot that moose!"

"Hey," he growled, "that moose is legal. Moose are good to eat!" He sighted down the barrel of his rifle.

Jeff grabbed Debra and was hurrying her to the car when they heard the gunshot. They turned to see the moose crumble into the water. Debra cried out. I could hear her telling friends back home: "See that beautiful bull moose in the photo? A typical Alaska hunter came up and shot him for dinner!"

Legal or not, you just don't shoot Bullwinkle.

The next day's events did nothing to change Debra's first impression of what Alaska is all about. Although our guests had a cabin rental on the Kenai River, their beds were so uncomfortable that they fought over who would get the floor.

It was two cranky fishermen who punched out early in the cold dawn to catch the early bite in their rented boat. They motored along the river until they found what looked like a good spot. With icy fingers, the couple anchored and pulled out the fishing gear. They were waiting for their first bite when, incredibly, breaking the silence of the wilderness, was the sound of music.

The sound drifted along the river with the morning mist. Wait a minute. Was that Johnny Mathis singing?

Now they could hear: "Chances are / Just because I wear a silly grin / the minute you..." As they puttered closer, they could see two big loudspeakers, one at each end of a stranger's fishing boat. The morning stillness was shattered by big-amp sound. The Mathis fan shouted a hearty "good morning" over the din and then pulled out a thermos of coffee and his fishing pole. He looked content.

Jeff and Debra put away their poles, pulled anchor, and made their escape. They could run, but they couldn't hide. They were steaming like a hot cup of coffee in cold air. No matter where they went, the sound of music carried along the water. Mr. M. could be heard most of the morning. He was everywhere. It was wilderness interrupted.

When Jeff and Debra returned to the bed and breakfast, Debra was livid. After three days, she knew who Alaskans were. They were vulgar, insensitive, and cruel. Their manners were terrible, they destroyed the peace with big loudspeakers in their boats, and nasty guys shot magnificent moose from the highway. That perception was one she would be sharing with her friends and family. Definitely not one I hope to see in the Alaska visitors guide.

* * *

The same summer, one of our guests encountered a homesteader whose behavior proved to be more like that of the Alaskans I know and love. We tend to be pretty laid back, and that includes the way we dress. A person can go just about anywhere in Anchorage in jeans and a clean T-shirt.

Our guest, Tony, was an accountant from Chicago and a spiffy dresser. When he appeared midevening in a polo shirt and creased khakis, he looked as tidy as entries on a ledger sheet. We nicknamed him "Chicago."

"I'm going for a hike," Tony announced. ("Dressed like that?" I wondered) Could we suggest a good trail, he asked. My husband gave him directions to a mountain destination. We were into our season of super-long days; it would be light most of the night. Still, it was after 9:00 p.m. I worried. It was a half-hour drive each way. No problem, Tony insisted, and he was gone.

Twenty minutes later, our guest had driven to the end of the road. When Tony got out of the car, he was surprised to see a few homesteads at the foot of the valley. As he slipped some bottled water into the pocket of his light windbreaker, he saw a man walking toward him from one of the cabins. "Hello there. Where ya headed?" asked the homesteader.

"Thought I'd head up the valley and cross over that low pass to the other side," Tony answered, pointing toward the low sun beginning its parallel slide across the tips of the mountains.

"Well, you better be careful. I've been seeing bear up there. You armed?"

"Uh, no, I'm not."

"Tell ya what, young man. You better borrow my gun just to be safe." The homesteader reached inside his jacket and pulled out a gun. A big one.

"Look, you just take this bear gun up with you, look around, and have a good time. Hopefully, you'll be alone up there. Those blackies can be mean. Just don't run away from them, whatever you do. Makes you look like dinner. When you get back, no need to come to the cabin. Just put the gun back under the seat of the truck. Be careful. Have a good walk."

Tony took the .357 Magnum, looked for a place to carry

20

it, and finally stuck it in the pocket of his khakis. He'd become "Chicago carrying concealed."

The next morning, Tony told us what happened. On the mountain, while climbing high through the pass, he had encountered a large sow and her two cubs. There was a bit of distance between the bear family and him. Tony stayed calm. He moved very slowly. He resisted the impulse to run like hell. Tony talked to the bears.

"Hey, mama bear, I'm just out here for a little nighttime walk, just like you and your babies," Tony said softly as he slowly moved aside, keeping his eyes averted.

The sow squinted at Tony a bit before giving a single snort and loping away with her cubs. When Tony could breathe again, he headed back down the mountain. He kept checking to make sure he wasn't being followed. He put the gun in the truck just as the homesteader had told him to do, and drove home.

The next day, Tony seemed more amazed at the homesteader's trust than having an encounter with bears. We weren't. Handing a loaded .357 to a stranger with an warning to be careful and put it back where it belongs?

Pure Alaska.

"Weren't you terrified?" I asked.

"It wasn't a big deal," Tony explained. "I learned how to handle a gun in the Marines."

"Well, guns have to be the last resort," I said. "Guns jam. People get excited and shoot themselves in the foot. Or worse."

Tony nodded.

"There's a terrible Alaska joke. One hiker says to another, 'Oh, I never worry about bears.' To which his friend says, 'Why is that?'"

"And the punch line?" Tony prompted.

"I never worry about bears, because I can outrun you."

"Not very funny," Tony said.

"OK then, how about a true story," I said. "When a misinformed tourist at Denali National Park found himself on the same trail as a bear, he dropped to the ground and assumed the fetal position."

"What happened?" Tony asked.

"It was pretty brutal. The tourist survived, but not before the bear whopped him a good one with a paw.

Now none of the guidebooks are telling people to lie down and play dead."

"What you did, Tony," I said, "talking to the bear and moving slow, was perfect."

"That mama bear gave me a bit of a rush," Tony admitted, "but she wasn't as scary as some of the humans I meet every day on the streets of Chicago."

Apples Baked in Port Wine

My husband and I enjoyed the baked apples we were served in a Napa Valley bed and breakfast. Since the owner was absent, I developed my own version. When I serve baked apples with pancakes or waffles, guests always have the same reaction: "I haven't eaten baked apples for years!"

> *4 red baking apples*
> *1/2 cup brown sugar*
> *1/4 cup nuts—pecans or walnuts*
> *1 tsp cinnamon*
> *2 tbsp light corn syrup*
> *1 tbsp butter*
> *1 cup port wine*
> *Heavy cream*

Carefully core apples—I use a melon baller.
Cut away a bit of the top of the apple and slice just enough from the bottom to set the apple firmly in a baking dish (without piercing the apple).
Combine the sugar, nuts, and cinnamon.
Stuff the mixture into the apples.
Baste with corn syrup, butter and wine.
Bake approximately one hour, 350 degrees.
Serve with cream (optional).

Serves four.

CHAPTER 3

Combat Fishing

The Lure of Fishing

When the salmon are running, the fishermen are elbow to elbow on the riverbank. The guy next to you whips his fishing rod back and gives a muscular heave-ho to really get that big-ass lure out there. On the way to its watery destination, the lure can make an abrupt stop in anything that sticks out, a tree branch, a dog, your nose. To remove the offending hardware, there's the quick yank with the rusty pliers technique. Not recommended. Or possibly the "cut one end off the hook and pull the other end on through" option. Very painful. As the last resort the local doctor in Soldotna performs minor surgery on fishermen. After the ordeal, he adds his new find to a corkboard in the waiting room. The corkboard displays both the lure and the body part from which the lure was extracted. His corkboard could be called the wincing wall.

Most Alaskans run a bed and breakfast; they just don't get paid for it. Alaska is a cool destination for friends and relatives, so when the tribe hits town, you find beds for them and cook a lot of big breakfasts.

Maybe they're dying to see you, but my guess is most of them expect you to take them fishing. Not only that, but when they get home, everyone wants to see a cooler full of Alaska seafood. And in this case, size matters.

Try this scenario: Uncle Bert flies back to Little Town, Nebraska. The folks are dying to see the pictures of his fish. Bert has a story and an excuse but no pictures of dead fish. What? You went all the way to Alaska and didn't catch a fish? What's wrong with you?

Now, I don't care how much money you've socked away up here; if you can't deliver good fishing for your guests, you won't get any respect. Everyone will know their northern relative is a loser.

You can't let that happen. Your fishing reputation back home is on the line. And if you don't own an airplane or a boat, you're going to have to use the public highway. That's the hitch. There is one road going in and out of

Anchorage. When the fish are running, we are all on the same highway. Running is what fish do; driving is what fishermen do.

When my own mother came, she said she'd heard you don't even need to hook 'em. The fish are so plentiful they'll jump ashore into your waiting arms. Or into the boat. Wherever, just to get away from the crowd in the river!

My mother had a reputation back in Oregon as a good steelhead fisherwoman. She knew all about fishing, lying about fishing, and rubbing it in when she outfished the good old boys on the river.

I really wanted to take my mom on a successful fishing trip, one she could brag about later. But she had already been skunked in Alaska several times. I needed a sure thing, so I bought two plane tickets to a fish camp across Cook Inlet. There we'd be, slaying fish together on a remote wild river.

Soon after, we found ourselves sitting in a fogged-up floatplane on Lake Spenard, waiting to taxi down the channel. Our pilot was wiping a peephole off the inside of the windshield with a Kleenex so he could see. I didn't want to be the one to scream: "How can you see? This isn't safe. Let me out of here!"

As the pilot pushed the stick forward, rain streaked by the windows, waves furrowed in front of us, the engine roared onto the step, and we were off. Mom's fingers were pressed deep into my shoulder. When I threw a look back over my shoulder to reassure her, she gave me a brave little smile.

Alexander Creek was a rain-shrouded hour away. As the plane dropped down through the trees, the pilot threaded the line of the river, and slammed the plane down. The engine screamed at full throttle as we dodged fishing boats. Coming in hot, they call it. The speed gives the pilot some control over a swollen river running with a heavy current. The pilot cut the engine and taxied to a small dock.

Mom and I wobbled out of the plane into a heavy rain and a clutch of welcoming fishermen. If you were a woman looking for a man and you weren't particular, this would be the place. A shave and a haircut might have made the men more appealing, but it would take longer to get rid of the old-bait smell. Much longer. Someone had been wiping his fish-egg hands on his jeans. After years around small boys who fish, I would recognize the smell anywhere.

I don't think these guys had seen a woman in a while. "Come on up to the lodge. We'll get you something to warm you right up. Where you from? How long are you staying?" Hands guided us up to a cozy-looking log building.

There's a saying around here: "The farther north you go, the better lookin' you get." I hadn't felt that popular since my husband went to the restroom and left me alone in a Kodiak bar full of fishermen.

We had warm cocoas in our hands and were just starting to get acquainted when we found out that this was only a pickup point. Our cabin was down the river. Probably just as well. The guys at the lodge looked disappointed as we left for the quick boat ride to our camp.

Our camp was a pretty log cabin in a leafy setting, a nice outdoor grill, and a boat with an engine tied to a dock in front. I got a quick tour of the outboard.

I didn't mention to the guide that I'd never run one in my life. I was depending on my observational skills and my mom's ability to handle the anchor.

It was still raining hard and we were drenched, but Mom couldn't wait to hit the river. I managed to lower the outboard down into the water, start it up in neutral, and engage first gear. Although the river wasn't very wide, it was intimidating. The rains had given it a bit of speed. I really didn't want the motor to die.

I put my hand on the throttle, gave it a turn, and gunned the boat into the heaving current – just like I knew what I was doing. We headed out through the stormy chop to the nearest salmon hole. Mom was snuggled down tight into her rain gear, but I could see her bright, excited eyes.

Mom and I expected to have a deep hole full of ignorant wilderness salmon waiting for us, but we were in for a big disappointment. A three-hundred-dollar plane ride had bought us a chance to fish intimately with the other guy. We could have driven our car to a local stream if we had wanted an experience this social.

There were at least a dozen boats ahead of us, lined up stern to bow. We got a big "Hullo there, little ladies" from the men as they maneuvered to make a gap big enough for us to get in line – that is, if we knew how to park a boat in a space that moves.

Parallel parking has always challenged me. The river current and the wind didn't improve my aim. And my poor mother was left to heft astern when I yelled, "Throw the anchor, NOW!" After our first try, the guys were less friendly, but they gave us lots of room.

Every forty-five minutes or so, Mom would throw me a pathetic look.

"Oh, no. You have to pee AGAIN?"

"Yes, dear. Sorry."

We'd pull the anchor, bump the boat in front of us and the boat in back of us, and beat it to shore, where I'd dig the propeller deep into the muddy bank, killing the motor as Mom headed for the bushes. Deep, deep into the bushes, where she eventually lost her hearing aid but preserved her modesty.

I wish I could tell you the fish gods rewarded a couple of determined wilderness women with a fat salmon. It would have been wonderful if Mom could have taken a cooler full of wild fish home for her winter's dinners.

We'd have taken pictures with the two of us proudly holding up our dripping salmon. She could have bragged to her friends back at the senior center. I'd have been her favorite daughter. But I'd have to lie to you.

What I did catch was something I'd been missing for a few years: having fun with my mother. She could jump into a boat, haul an anchor, and laugh at the rain. I just couldn't believe how tough she was. She was seventy-five that year and still the queen of the river to me.

* * *

When a retired senator from Georgia and his young grandson showed up at the bed and breakfast one summer day, fishing poles in hand, and said they wanted to go fishing, I didn't hold much hope for them. They didn't have a car or much time, just tomorrow. Still, when faced with a young boy's enthusiasm, you try a little harder.

That night, the senator, his grandson, and my husband talked fishing. What else? Everyone got excited. My husband had an idea. Since they didn't have a car, why not try fishing downtown in Ship Creek?

I consider Ship Creek to be a big mud hole. It's down

at the Port of Anchorage, where the land fell in during the 1964 earthquake. The extreme tides wash glacial silt in and out of the mouth of Ship Creek. The local fishermen slip and slide down a steep riverbank for an urban assault on the salmon.

It's also possible to get stuck in the goopy mess and to have to wait for the Jaws of Life to rescue you before the tide comes in. If you're lucky. On the plus side, it's a one-minute climb up the bank to a hot dog and a latte. There is that.

My cynical remarks about the creek didn't seem to matter to our guests. They weren't here for the aesthetics. This boy was here to fish, and the silvers were running.

Early the next morning, my husband was going to drive the senator and his grandson to the creek. Since it was spitting rain, the first stop they'd make would be at the Army surplus store. They needed slickers and rubber boots. As I watched them go, I felt sorry for them. They were going to get wet, tired, dirty, and discouraged.

However, when we came in late that evening, I was surprised to see an empty box of plastic Baggies. Was there something in the freezer?

Before breakfast the next morning, an excited young-ster told his story. He and his grandpa had arrived at Ship Creek just as the tide was coming in. They must have looked somewhat lost because some of the locals got out of their folding chairs, put their plastic ponchos aside, and gave the newcomers the hospitality of the river.

They showed them how to rig their line with salmon eggs. Demonstrated how and where to cast. Told them what to do when they got a strike. Offered the senator some whiskey.

I have a dimly formed theory about boys and fishing karma.

First, when a boy throws out a line, a fish doesn't smell Irish Spring or Dial soap on the lure. Just dirty fish-bait hands, stiff sock aroma – natural boy smell. Fish love it.

Second, a boy expects to catch a fish. While the rest of us are getting bored or eating our lunch, a boy is al-ways ready for that sudden jerk on the pole. He imagines the fish swimming along, the fish seeing the lure, the fish striking the lure. Then, BOOM!

On the bank, the good 'ole boys and the senator were

busy exchanging fishing stories. His grandson was antici-
pating. Suddenly a silver struck. The tip of his pole dipped
toward the muddy ground.

"I got a fish, Grandpa."

"Set the hook."

"Don't horse it."

"Keep your tip up!"

Cries went up as nearby fishermen reeled in their
lines to get out of the way. It was a noble battle, but
25-pound-test line usually does the trick. At last, a tired
young fisherman dragged a flopping salmon up the muddy bank. A net appeared, the prize was snared, and the
day and the fish belonged to a boy from Georgia.

How were the senator and his grandson going to get
their big salmon home? Like everything else that day, they
figured it out with some help from friendly Alaskans. Plastic and duct tape works for almost any situation.

I have an image of the senator and his grandson sitting
on the bench seat of the No. 33 city bus, headed home
with their silver salmon stashed in a donated plastic gar-
bage bag, its tail protruding out the top.

Everyone on the bus wanted to know where the fish came from. It had to be exciting for the boy to tell about the battle of Ship Creek. Many of the people on the bus had their own fish stories. A warm, steamy bus ride, good company, a really big fish. It must have been a proud moment. When the senator's grandson talked about it, you could tell how happy he was. He came, he saw, and he caught one. He believed.

Now the fish was frozen and packed in an extra suitcase for the trip back to Georgia. There were warm hugs and, finally, goodbyes.

I always feel a bit wistful when the house gets quiet again. After they left, I imagined what form the story would take by the time they got back home. I picked up the guest book to read their comments while I drank one more cup of coffee. The senator's name was in the book. Underneath it, our young fisherman had written his name and in his child's script: "Fish caught, Ship Creek, 24 inches, silver salmon on salmon eggs."

Every boy should get a chance to land a twenty-four-incher. And as happy as the Georgia schoolboy was, I'd bet my tackle box the big whoop of the day belonged to the senator. Even though I love to feel a big yank on my line, knowing dinner is on the other end; I would have traded every future catch of the day to have seen my mother haul in a big one on Alexander Creek. Eight or eighty, the big ones belong to them.

Fruity French Toast

Everyone enjoys this satisfying breakfast. I assemble the dish the night before and bake it the next morning while guests are showering. I like to present it on a trivet at the table. It may fall a bit, but it will be just as delicious.

> *1 large loaf of French bread*
> *(cut into 1-1/2-inch slices)*
> *6 eggs*
> *1-1/2 cup half and half*
> *1 tsp vanilla*
> *1/4 tsp cinnamon*
> *1/4 tsp nutmeg*
> *Fresh blueberries or raspberries*
> *Topping*
> *1/4 cup butter*
> *1/2 cup brown sugar*
> *1 tbsp corn syrup*

Beat eggs, half and half, vanilla, and spices together. Pour over bread slices and refrigerate.

In the morning, press the fruit gently into any little crevices between bread slices.

Microwave topping ingredients for about 1 minute, then pour or spread gently over the bread and fruit.

Bake at 350 for about half an hour, until lightly browned.

Serve with fresh whipped cream (optional).

Serves four to six.

CHAPTER 4

Looking for a Good Man

She came with one piece of luggage and a copy of Alaska Men magazine under her arm. "Hi, I'm Cindy," she said with a friendly smile. Cindy wore a bulky, long turtleneck sweater over a short skirt. Other than her pretty knees, she looked like the rest of us. Laugh lines and a few extra pounds.

"I can't believe I'm really on vacation," Cindy said. "I left a 12-year-old daughter back home in Denver. Feels so funny to be here without her."

"Well, that's what phone cards are for," I replied.

"Yeah," I've been instructed to call her at least once a day. She's worried. I've been writing and e-mailing some guys in this magazine," she said with a laugh. I'm here to meet a few of them in person. Pretty brave, aren't I?"

That's when I first heard Cindy's laugh. A sort of rising

bubble that frothed up and spilled out, like champagne in a glass, very light. Her enthusiasm carried me along with her. This gal isn't desperate and dateless, I thought. She's adventurous. How interesting.

"I'm going to meet one of the guys," she said, waving her magazine at me as I showed her to her room. I'll keep you posted on how it goes."

"Be careful, kid," I said. "There's some desperation out there. I was reading an ad in the personals last week, strictly for entertainment, you understand. One of the ads read: 'Mountain climber, interested in meeting petite blonde for harness action.' See what I mean?"

"Sure, sure," Cindy said. "Take a look at page fourteen," she added, laughing again as she handed me her magazine.

Thumbing through, I had to admit these were rugged-looking guys. Here were a musher in a heavy parka and a beard, a man fly-fishing, a fireman featured on a calendar with eleven more of Anchorage's finest, a cutie looking up at me from his sleeping bag, and a woodsy-looking guy standing outside his cabin. Whoa, full menu!

They all looked good in jeans and flannels, no suits here. Maybe these guys would look like outdoor types anywhere; however, when an Alaska man says he likes "long walks on the beach," that might translate to "I have a Visqueen tent with a blue tarp for a door. It's a long walk on the beach to get to it." "Enjoys a quiet, candlelight dinner" might mean "There's no electricity in my cabin."

Women Outside find Alaska men fascinating enough to subscribe to a magazine advertising bachelors, but I say: "Buyer, beware! There's definitely something to the local cliché 'The odds are good, but the goods are odd.'"

Obviously, Cindy had a well-developed sense of adventure. She promised to keep me posted on what was happening. Thank goodness. My nose would have gotten caught in the door.

Cindy was to meet her first contact at a bar called Chilkoot Charlie's, locally known as Koots. Now, Koots is a serious bar: loud music, Alaska brew, fights. Singles love the place. Something's happening. And as the bar's ads brag: "We cheat the other guy and pass the savings on to you."

When Cindy walked into Koots, a man walked across the room to greet her. He looked better than his picture. He was straight out of a Coors ad, with rugged good looks. "God bless your mom and dad," she thought. "Good job!"

"It was so exciting to be excited about a guy," Cindy told me later. "We sat down and ordered a beer, but all he did was talk about himself. Talky, talky, talky. Finally, he did ask me one question: "How do you feel about hookin' up on the first date?"

"You know what I did?" Cindy said. "I gave the big dork a fetchin' smile, picked up my purse, and said: 'Gotta go to the girls' room. Be right back.' I used my cell phone to call a cab, found the backdoor exit, and just kept walking!"

"Hey, I won't worry about you anymore, girl. You rock!"

"Darn, he was so good-looking too."

When I lifted my arms and gestured for the chorus to sing, Cindy joined me in the chant "THE GOODS ARE ODD."

Later in the day, I could hear Cindy talking to her daughter, Holly, on the phone. "No," she said, "you don't have a new daddy. I'm just getting to know some people. Don't worry, hon."

42

I could relate to Holly's anxious questions. My father died young, and after that, my mother always had a bright optimism that she would find real love again. The morning after Mom had "gone out," her breath would smell of cigarette smoke and bourbon. She would tell me what she had for dinner, the men she met. She brought me multi-colored swizzle sticks and little paper umbrellas from her drinks. I loved hearing about her nightlife. But I worried about what kind of guy she might bring home. How he might change our lives.

As an adult, I heard that some of Dad's family criticized my mother. Called her unfit. I guess that was because she was gone at night a lot. But I never asked questions. She was my mother. I loved her. Even though she was susceptible to heart-breaking hunky types who were just passing through, every morning was a fresh new day for my mother.

When Cindy and Holly talked on the phone, I could hear the same kind of mother-daughter intimacy I had known as a girl. I could picture Holly, a precocious little girl on the other end of the line saying, "Do I have a new father?" And Cindy's laughing reply, "Not yet, sweetie."

For the next few days, Cindy was busy, busy making dates with her boyfriend pen pals. After the first day, if the phone rang, it was usually for Cindy.

Cindy was hopeful about a man she had written to for several months. They planned to meet for pizza at four in the afternoon. Here he was now, walking toward her. Cute smile, friendly face. Then he opened his mouth.

"Hey, great blouse. Did you buy it at a garage sale? Ha ha ha, I see a guy I got to talk to for a minute. Why don't you go ahead and get a beer. I'll be right back."

Ten minutes later, he sat down beside her in a booth, all chatty and friendly. And in spite of the rude beginning, she found she kind of liked the guy. He had great energy and his blue eyes snapped with intensity. He asked her about herself and seemed interested.

But there was that joke about her eighty-dollar silk blouse. She had to buy her own beer. And he bought the pizza with a coupon. The goods are odd. Cindy crossed him off her list.

I didn't worry when Cindy took off one morning with a man she had exchanged e-mail with. I actually knew her new friend, a nice guy who mined for gold in summer and did "this and that" in winter. Wilderness bachelor? This guy was the real thing.

Cindy would get to see the cabin he'd been working on for seven years, the one with moose antlers nailed over the front door and an old Ford F-150 parked in the back. There were a couple of wrecks out there too, in case he needed spare parts for the truck. He lived with a wolf-dog hybrid called Yukon.

Last time I talked to him, he didn't have running water or lights but managed to have a morning latte. He'd rigged a small espresso maker to his truck battery. Hey, do what's important!

When Cindy got home that night, she just shook her head no at me. When she talked to Holly that evening, she sounded tired.

Cindy had one more day before she left. She was going to spend it on a rafting trip down the Matanuska River. The river is only about an hour from Anchorage, and it has some world-class white water.

Cindy was wild-eyed when she checked in with me,

much later. She had shared the raft with some Swiss mountain climbers. The whole team, in fact. There'd been white-water rapids, blue skies, and thrills and chills with hunky men in wet T-shirts. Yes!

It was screamingly scary going down the river rapids. She was so afraid that she had to hold on to the guys. Too bad. Once safely ashore, they all had a small celebratory nip. The guys offered to run the river again with Cindy as their guest. She was up for it. I'm a little unclear what happened on the second trip, but I think Cindy lost her inhibitions and her T-shirt!

When the week was over, I was sorry to see Cindy go. I was old enough to be Cindy's mom, but when she talked to Holly, I was a little girl again, talking with my own mother. For weeks after Cindy left, the phone continued to ring. Everyone wanted to talk to Cindy.

The question is why. There are plenty of women in Anchorage who are home alone. Why was Cindy so popular? She was at the bed and breakfast every night, not warming a bed somewhere else.

Theory. Maybe everyone wanted her time because Cindy

had the ultimate attraction. She still liked men. No bitter "I hate men, post-divorce, men-are-pigs" attitude. Even though she didn't meet someone she wanted to take home to be Holly's new daddy, she'd had a great time. I don't think the word "discouraged" was in Cindy's vocabulary.

If a woman wants a good man, she can probably find one in Sheboygan or Spokane or wherever she calls home. For summer fun, Alaska's a great place for a feisty, independent woman.

If you do make a trip north, be sure to pack Cindy's big, break-your-face smile and a belief that a new day might bring love or a laugh or at least a wet ride down a fast river.

Caramelized French Toast with Pecans

This is a rich French toast reminiscent of pecan pie. It's delicious served with breakfast sausage. I always give my full attention when caramelizing the toast, as it can burn easily.

> *French bread cut into 1-inch slices*
> *4 eggs*
> *1 cup milk*
> *1 tsp vanilla*
> *1/2 cup brown sugar*
> *1 tbsp light oil*
> *1 tbsp butter*
> *1/2 cup pecans*
> *Whipped cream (optional)*

Beat eggs and milk with vanilla.
Soak bread slices in egg mixture while heating oil in heavy skillet.
In skillet, brown bread on both sides until light golden.
Transfer bread to a heated serving platter.
Add butter to the pan and melt on medium high heat.
Add brown sugar and stir to caramelize.
Return French toast to pan and quickly coat both sides in caramel.
Transfer to platter.
Toast pecans quickly in remaining caramel.
Sprinkle toasted pecans over toast.
Serve with maple syrup and whipped cream.

Serves four to six.

CHAPTER 5

Keepin' 'Em Safe
In Loco Parentis

Early one spring, a small sparrow

Nestled in a lilac bush

Growing close to

Our big dining room window.

I had a perfect

Day-to-day view of

Four tiny blue eggs

In a diminutive nest.

The little sparrow sat stolidly in her nest,

Buffeted wildly about

By spring wind and rain.

Soon eggs became chicks.

As they grew, they became voracious.

When the mother sparrow

Tried to feed them,

They knocked her out of the nest.

Finally, she sneaked up a branch,

And leaped over the edge

To avoid being pushed

Out by big-mouthed chicks.

Take, take, take!

As I showered one morning,

There was bedlam

Outside my window,

Loud cheeping and bird noises,

Then silence.

I grabbed a towel

And ran to the window

To check on the chicks.

They were gone.

I never had children of my own.

What I don't know about kids is a lot.

And although children aren't chicks,

I bet they are alike in one way:

Take, take, take.

A house could get quiet

Without the "Gimmee, gimmee."

Of a child.

I felt loss when the sparrow

Family flew away.

I understood why some call

That empty feeling

A syndrome.

—Sherry Tomlinson—

As a bed and breakfast hostess, I can continue my lifelong role of mothering other people's kids. After twenty-plus years of teaching high school, I still get to "hang" with young people. We host students under the age of twenty who are on their way to a month long school in wilderness skills. Some will be canoeing in Prince William Sound, others backpacking in the Talkeetna Mountains, or perhaps climbing Denali Mountain. My husband and I consider ourselves "in loco parentis," legalese meaning: We fill in for their real parents.

I get lots of phone calls from parents. We talk about what kind of trouble their kids might find in the big, bad town of Anchorage. Parents have real-world worries, but I don't think that's what makes them clingy. Their kids could get into trouble in Anchorage, same as anywhere else, but anywhere else isn't a long airplane ride and a month away. No phones, letters, or e-mail. For a month, their child will be off the leash.

Mostly, parents ask about drugs. If kids want to find drugs, the store is open in Alaska. With no experience in recreational chemistry, I don't make a good drug czarina. As a teacher in a high school classroom, students asked me about drug use when I was a kid. I don't think they believed me when I told them that if drugs were around, they were invisible.

When I was a teen in health class, we were shown a movie called "Reefer Madness." Crazy kids went from a single drag on a marijuana cigarette to becoming full-blown heroin addicts. From fun to death in a fast-frame. It was a silly film, but it scared me right into trying alcohol.

I was also terrified of getting pregnant, the H-bomb, and not being popular. Maybe if marijuana had been around, I might have smoked it, who knows? As it is, I wouldn't know pot from oregano.

One morning when housekeeping, I discovered a curious-looking little gizmo in a sixteen-year-old guest's room. The object was a small pipe with a mouthpiece attached to it. My guest had walked to town, so I couldn't ask him what it was. When I showed it to my husband later, he didn't hesitate: "Oh, that's a bong."

"A bong?" I asked. "What's a bong?"

"Dope," he replied. "The pipe's for smoking dope."

My mother hen's feathers went into full fluff as I screeched: "WHAT? He was smoking pot? That's terrible. He could set the house on fire. What will his parents say? I won't stand for it. NOT IN THIS HOUSE!"

You get the picture. Over the edge. Reefer madness!

My husband, who is a street-smart guy, spoke in calm tones to me: "Honey, get a grip. This kid thought he had some privacy. He's going to be as shocked as you. Don't put him in a no-win situation that's going to make you both unhappy."

"But what if he does it again?" I protested. "I WON'T HAVE IT!"

"Settle down, sweetheart. He's not going to do it again. Here's what I suggest you do. Write a note. Explain that you expect him to get rid of his drug stuff. Ask him to please respect the rules of a drug-free house. Put it with the bong, where he can see it."

After fuming a bit more, I figured my husband was probably right. I did as he suggested. For a change. Evening came and went. Nothing was said. Nary a ripple on the serene surface of the home pond.

The next morning, I served waffles and sweetness to my pot-smoking guest. There was syrup on the table too. Neither of us was talking about it. Soon after breakfast, my guest left, off to the wilderness. Nice knowing you.

While housekeeping later, I discovered a note on the table next to my guest's bed: "I apologize to you and your husband. I did not mean to show disrespect in your house. Thank you for being kind. I left you a present. Have a good time."

On the table where the note had been was a half-empty bottle of tequila.

* * *

I felt like a mother hen the day a taxi brought another wilderness student to our front door. She was sixteen and nearly six feet tall. Trish was a strong-looking girl with a gorgeous Zena, Warrior Princess-type figure. She wore no makeup, just a healthy, friendly smile. When Trish walked, she looked like an invitation.

Of course, taking a walk downtown to see what was happening was just what a young girl would want to do on a perfect June day. In spite of my misgivings, I sent Trish on her way with a lecture about talking to strangers and coming home early. But curfews can be a tough sell here in Alaska. With more hours of daylight, there's more time to get into trouble.

When Trish returned a few hours later, she'd had a phone call. "It's from the guy you sat next to on the airplane," I explained as I handed her a sticky note.

The phone rang again. Someone she'd met at a downtown gift shop wanted to chat.

55

Another call, another young man she'd met on the trail. "He'd like to take me to dinner. What do you think?" she asked. Good girl.

I really wanted to disconnect the phone, but I went for damage control instead. "Have your friend grab a pizza. There are Cokes in the fridge. Invite him over. He can visit you here."

It worked. He turned out to be a sweetheart, well-mannered, asking politely if I minded if they watched TV in Trish's room. Since there is no television in the living room, it seemed like an OK deal. My husband and I gave them privacy, but we were around. Parents would understand the maneuver.

Later, when I went into the kitchen for a snack, I didn't like what I saw. Trish's bedroom door was open, the TV was on, and there were two pairs of feet toes up, side-by-side on the queen bed.

What to do? March into the room and break it up? I thought it over. I didn't want to embarrass anyone. The door was open and, all four feet were pointing up.

I decided to create an amiable diversion. Clattering

56

loudly around the kitchen, I soon had some brownies in the oven. As the brownies were baking, the double-chocolate smell got them off the bed, out of the bedroom and into the kitchen. Brilliant!

* * *

When students arrive here as guests, they can be nervous. They will be tested in some of the wildest country left on earth. They won't have fast food, a cell phone, a shower, or, more importantly, toilet paper. What they do have, when they return, is a new knowledge of how to be safe in the outdoors.

We were surprised when we had a seventeen-year-old student return from his kayaking trip two weeks early. An accident in his kayak left him with deep lacerations and ugly bruises. He hadn't been hospitalized, but he needed time for his body to mend. With big gashes on his shoulder and leg, he needed some TLC before returning home.

Our guest had been kayaking near an ocean shore in Prince William Sound. He must have been feeling a little cocky, because he started practicing rollovers. In a rollover, a kayaker swings himself and his boat under the water, using the momentum of the roll to pop back up to the surface. Not a smart maneuver in frigid Alaska waters. The student didn't realize the sea bottom was filled with boulders. He was young, invincible, and alone.

On his second roll, his head made contact with a rock. He was momentarily stunned and head down in water just barely above freezing.

I know what it's like to be in water that cold. I once fell headfirst into a deep creek. The cold water hit me like a sledgehammer. For a few panicked moments, I couldn't think or act. Finally, I swam for what I hoped was up.

The kayaker would have been similarly disoriented. He wouldn't have the strength or the momentum of the roll to right himself.

Fortunately, another student paddled by the cove, happened to look over, and saw the overturned kayak. He paddled hard toward the kayak, hoping to find his teammate alive.

Mustering his strength, he was able to turn the water-filled kayak over with the student still in it, manage his own boat, and haul for shore. Pulling the victim out of the kayak and onto the beach, He knew he had to get his colleague warm. Fast. His buddy would be in shock. There was a lot of blood dripping from his head wound.

After stripping his clothes off, the rescuer used his wilderness training to battle the inevitable hypothermia. He exchanged the student's wet clothing with his own dry ones. Wearing the wet clothing now, he covered the nearly unconscious kayaker with a tarp and called for help. Rescue was a radiophone call and a helicopter ride away. God bless modern technology.

Later, the injured youngster was to say to me: "I was pulled out by the only person in the group strong enough to do it. It took a crack on the head for me to get smart. I know how lucky I am."

When out playing in the Alaska wilderness, you don't often get a second mistake.

* * *

When students return from trips safely, I'm happy to see them. They get to the bed and breakfast and say, "It's so good to be home." They sleep in a feather bed, take long soaks in the hot tub, and spend time with a fill-in mom who will cook for them and listen to their stories.

When they come back, they feel ten feet tall. They have a fancy certificate of completion. They've learned to cook, plan, and play well with others. The skills they have acquired will probably serve them well in the urban wilderness they're going home to.

Returnees don't want to talk about mountain adventures; they want to talk about food. They share their recipes, special dishes like pizza made from Bisquick, chocolate chips, and tomato sauce, all topped with any dried whatevers they have left. Over the month, they've eaten lots of pasta. They have not been starving, but they've had to ration their food. It must give new meaning to an excellent old prayer, "Give us this day our daily bread."

Last summer, after a month of mountaineering, two tall, thin New York college boys sat at the breakfast bar and watched me cook. They had eyes only for me, or rather for the breakfast I was putting together. They ate a huge meal of meat, eggs, and potatoes with a basket of muffins on the side and a pitcher full of fruit smoothie. I was being sarcastic when I asked if they'd like some pancakes to top it off. "Great idea!" they chorused. Tweedledee and Tweedledum. No one on the Atkins diet around here.

I warn students that when they go home, it will be a little like returning from a war. Their friends' concerns may seem trite and urban noise overwhelming. It will be hard for their friends and families to understand what it means to be on your own in the wilderness, where you may be bailed out if the situation turns dangerous, but your rescuer is going to have to be a hero. Or that food, warmth, shelter, and dry underwear will never again be taken for granted.

Like little snowbirds, students leave our protection to migrate back south, where now know how to take care of themselves and make a great-tasting pizza.

Smoked Salmon Omelet

This is my version of a delicious salmon omelet I had the pleasure of eating in a Parisian bistro. I'm sure the eggs were cooked quickly on a flat grill. Lacking a restaurant-style stove, I improvise by using my largest flat-bottomed skillet. It is important to present this elegant omelet on a warm plate. Serve with lightly toasted French bread and warm preserves.

> 4 very thin slices of raw smoked salmon
> (or lox)
> Butter and oil
> 6 eggs
> Salt, pepper to taste
> Fresh dill and/or chives
> Sour cream (lite or regular)

Rough chop herbs and warm the plates.

Heat a thin layer of butter and oil in large skillet. Be careful not to scorch.

Froth eggs with salt and pepper.

Pour eggs into skillet. The omelet should be thin enough to heat quickly but thick enough to support the weight of the salmon.

Shake eggs gently over medium heat until they are nearly set. Place one slice of salmon in center of omelet.

Fold sides over onto the center, making a square. Lay the last salmon slice on top.

Transfer omelet to warm plate. The salmon slice enclosed

within the omelet will be cooked, the top slice raw but warm.

Repeat for second omelet. Sprinkle herbs on top and serve with a dollop of sour cream.

Serves four.

CHAPTER 6

Lovers, Virginity, and Beds

There's a four-way stop in front of our house. As I work at my computer and look out the window, I've learned that a stop sign is, to most people, merely a suggestion. For some, it means slow down, don't stop. Then there's the pedal-to-the-metal mentality exhibited by the doofus who not only runs the sign but actually accelerates through it.

For me, a stop sign can be the pause that refreshes. My mind fetches up on some fluffy mental cloud, and I just sit there and forget to "Go."

Maybe love can be a four-corner decision. Some lovers are cautious, some crash and burn, and some just sit there, until someone behind them honks his horn.

There is a wet moment in the film "Bridges of Madison County" when Meryl Streep and her husband sit in their truck at an intersection, windshield wipers whisking away a heavy rain. Clint Eastwood is sitting in his car in front of them. When the light says "Go," he doesn't. Meryl's hand clutches the door handle. All time stops and the future whirls on that focused moment when Meryl must decide whether to stay with her husband or go with Clint. I get misty just thinking about it.

I was to be reminded of that movie moment once when a couple stayed with us for a few days before getting married on Sunday. At the breakfast table, I asked them a question guaranteed to bring life to a conversation. "How did you two meet?"

Wes and Ellen were eager to answer. They wanted to rehearse their story before telling it at their wedding day celebration. They told me that not only had their lives crossed each other's at a critical intersection but that their path had crossed mine as well.

Wes and Ellen found each other at a great place to meet other thirty-somethings, a folk dance group. He had a masculine, direct way about him. Dark eyes, lean build. She had an athlete's physique and soft eyes. Between dances, they discovered they were both avid long-distance cyclists. Wes had biked across Europe. After a bike tour across the contiguous United States and then Alaska, Ellen had plunked herself down permanently in Anchorage. The two of them had a lot to talk about. Wes thought things were working. Not only was she pretty, she was nice.

Wes made his move. "Let's do some cycling together sometime. Here's my phone number; call me."

"That's different," Ellen replied. "Doesn't the guy usually say, 'I'll call you'?"

"Yeah, but when a guy says it, it usually means good-bye. I'm asking you to decide, Ellen. Maybe when you want to say hello, you'll call."

I loved it! For a change, the man was sitting by the phone, waiting for it to ring.

After three weeks, Ellen gave Wes a call. "I liked his approach," she said.

In the movies, when a couple falls in love, there's a typical sequence in which they play, tease, feed each other funny food, make love, and laugh and laugh, all in soft focus. I'm imagining that in Wes and Ellen's case, there was also a lot of biking.

For a year they were a couple on their way to a decision about their future. Then Wes braked. He had an opportunity to go on an extended bike trip in Europe, and he took it.

A year later, Wes came back. He had pictures and a year's worth of stories. He also had an unpleasant surprise waiting for him. While he was having his adventure, Ellen's wheels had turned in another direction. She wanted to make progress in her career, explore possibilities, become more herself, and, in those devastating words, just be friends.

He was destroyed by her decision. As the groom told their story over a plateful of pancakes and fruit, he stopped to use his napkin on his eyes. He told of his mourning over the next three years. Though he lost track of Ellen, he couldn't forget her. His friends were understanding at first, then started to avoid him, and, finally, suggested he "seek help." For Wes, this wasn't just a breakup. It was a serious breaking of the heart.

Wes needed to see Ellen one more time. He felt if he could just have one last talk with her, he could heal himself. Over and over, he rehearsed the conversation he would have with her. Then Wes talked to Ellen in a dream.

You have to believe in the good dreams. I think some dreams are just mental junk, like when you dream you are putting price tags on stuff when you've been working retail all day. Some dreams are fun, like sex and flying.

Some dreams speak to you. Like a Freudian wish-fulfillment dream. You talked to your dead grandmother. Or you realize that you are in love with the guy in the third-row seat in biology class. The kind of dream that when you wake up, you know something you didn't know when you went to sleep.

I think Wes had that kind of dream. He absolutely knew he would see Ellen again.

Soon after that, Wes was biking on Anchorage's coastal trail when he thought he saw Ellen jogging through the rain. He stopped and looked after her as she ran by him. He went to the nearest park bench and sat down, heart pounding, waiting, hoping she would turn around.

He watched her run to the trail stop sign and pause. She stood there, not moving. Perhaps she was balancing the future in a moment, like a raindrop suspended on a windshield.

Suddenly, there she was. "Hello again, Wes," she said softly as she sat next to him on the bench.

It was happening just as he had dreamed it would. As his eyes met hers, he was aware of the rain washing over her face, the rain glistening on her bare legs, the rain running down his own neck. He was glued to her presence, but he couldn't speak. His fantasy conversations of "She said to me" and then "I said to her" just lodged in his throat.

"It's been almost three years, Wes, since we've seen each other. We should've run into each other before now on the trails. You'd think so, anyway. So where have you been?"

"I waited for you to call," he blurted. "I wanted you to make the first move, Ellen. Like before."

"I'm so sorry. I didn't know how to tell you I wasn't ready. Things seemed to go forward so fast. I could have been kinder."

"I don't know, Ellen. Who does breakups right?"

"Yeah, well, I've got to go." She rose to leave. "It's not getting any drier here."

"Wait, Ellen. I want us to talk. Meet me for coffee in the

morning. I don't need more than that right now."

"Just talk? That's it?"

"Just talk. Promise."

"I'll think about it. Maybe I'll call, Wes."

I'm only imagining the lovers' conversation, but Wes must have found the magic words to say because Wes and Ellen were here, eating breakfast with a surprise for me.

Their stay with us was no accident.

One day Wes and Ellen were out walking in the park. They sat down on the same bench where Wes had waited for Ellen. As they looked across the park, Ellen spotted a small sign. "Wes, it's a bed and breakfast. Let's honeymoon there. It would be perfect."

I just finished making a wedding card for my newly married guests. The picture on the card shows two red bikes leaning against a flowering tree alongside a forest pathway. Inside the card, I've wished them a good journey and a fair wind at their back. I hope they like it.

When I was working on the card, I thought about lovers, how fragile they are. When Wes and Ellen were talking, I guess they learned to listen to each other.

They were a fun couple to watch. When Ellen was telling her version of their courtship, Wes's eyes would catch hers and then light up with enjoyment. I could see in Wes's face that Ellen was his baby-doll. When he talked, her face followed the rhythm of his words like a dance partner. All could have been lost on a pivot. When Ellen got to that stop sign, it might have been easier for her to keep going. But unlike Meryl, the lady opened the door and jumped.

* * *

At this bed and breakfast, I'm the maid. And even though I have work to do in a guest's bedroom, I can still feel shy when entering. There's often a lingering warm-nest smell from the night's sleep. It feels a bit like invading someone's privacy. When cleaning, I refold, replace, refresh, and then get out.

However, with one young Midwestern couple, I became an unwitting bedroom anthropologist. My guests, Lucy and Joe, had been married the day before they took the long flight to Alaska. Lucy had curly hair that bounced with animation when she talked. No tattoos, nose rings, or naked midriff. Just an unusually sweet expression in her dark eyes. Joe was a fresh-faced rancher with a congenial manner. They had the sort of heartland openness that seems to flourish within a family who works hard together.

They were excited to be in Alaska and folded me into their enthusiasm. They snapped and sparked with questions, and I shot answers back at them. Yes, we do get moose in our yard. Yes, those are Alaska blueberries in your pancakes and reindeer in your sausage. Yes, bears do kill people but usually don't eat them.

By the time we chatted through several long breakfasts, it felt like saying goodbye to my own kids. They had purchased a mini-tour from an inn-sized bed and breakfast in the downtown area. A bus would take them forty miles south for a quick train ride to Whittier and, finally, a fabulous glacier cruise on Prince William Sound.

I gave them a lift. We parked at the bed and breakfast inn with fifteen minutes to spare, but there was no bus waiting for them in the parking lot. The newlyweds wilted with disappointment. Inexperienced and shy, they weren't sure what to do.

I volunteered to go into the place and find out what was going on. An unfriendly woman looked through a cigarette-smoke cloud and gave me the rude news: "The bus left fifteen minutes early."

"What? You didn't wait for prepaid guests?"

"Sorry. The bus was ready to go."

My guests had been charged for a ride they didn't get.

Now, I think of myself as a gentle woman, patient and kind. However, as a retired high school teacher, I can still deliver what my students described as "the psycho look." Think John Travolta in "Get Shorty." Don't blink.

With a steady stare and a soft voice, I introduced myself to the desk clerk as a fellow bed and breakfast owner, a member of hospitality organizations, and a person who likes to write letters to the editor. Pay up or pay the penalty. My eyes were starting to water from the smoke circling up from the clerk's cigarette. But I didn't blink.

I walked out of the inn with a refund in my hand. Lucy and Joe were grateful, but they still had a problem. They were going to miss their 12:00 train to Whittier if they didn't leave now. The solution was obvious. I lent them my car. It seemed like the best thing to do.

I hugged the honeymooners and gave them my traveler's blessing: "Keep your headlights on, be safe, and don't forget to floss."

Later, as I was cleaning the room they had occupied, I saw something that made me stop stripping the bed. The sheets in my hands had the stains of a marriage's first night. Lucy had been a virgin.

I plunked myself down on the edge of the bed, astonished. Do people still wait until marriage to have sex? There are honest-to-goodness virgins walking around out there?

When I was a young woman, virginity or lack of it defined us. You were a good girl or the other kind. There was no sexual freedom, just guilt. Somewhere in the 1960s, I assumed everyone joined the sexual revolution. Sweet surprise. Instead of "Sex and the City," this couple came from "Little House on the Prairie." The thought left me wrapped in a sort of amazement.

I thought of old England and imagined the clan and other hang-abouts assembled below the bedroom balcony to view the display of bed sheets from a royal marriage.

The linen was waved as proof that both bride and paternity had been intact.

As I changed these sheets, I felt like a young woman's handmaiden in a place long ago and far away, where bridal white was more than a fashion statement.

I imagined that the honeymoon couple would now be driving through the raw beauty of Turnagain Arm on their way to Whittier. They would see deep glacial valleys; forest green with a backdrop of sharp peaks, still creamy with a glaze of last winter's melting snow. The mountainsides would be hanging gardens, the brushy white goat's beard bowing in the wind, the earthquake-drowned mudflats of Cook Inlet resurrected in acres of blue lupine, and bouquets of wildflowers tucked into rocky crevasses.

The mountain-hugging drive offers up-close views of wildlife—eagles fishing, sheep, and spring lambs seemingly posing very near the salt-sprinkled highway—and my favorite, beluga whales. Their gleaming backs show as white crescents in the glacially fed waters of the inlet as the whales feed on tiny oily hooligan.

On a warm summer afternoon like this one, cars, RVs,

and busses would be parked anywhere they could. If the tides are right, the couple might see one of the world's most dramatic tidal bores as tide, wind, and water pile up the waves in the narrowing channel. And not a sign or billboard or taco stand blocking the view.

The honeymooners were seeing that bit of paradise in my car. My gift to a couple who believed in being the first one. The thought of the old-fashioned lovers warmed my heart.

* * *

The most important word in "bed and breakfast" is "bed." When I'm a guest shown to my room, I drop my luggage, look around, lie down on the bed, and do a snow angel in the covers. A bed should be a cozy refuge from the challenges of travel. It should whisper, "You are safe."

One day while looking through a glossy magazine, I was captivated by a lavish bed in an advertisement. A gorgeous young couple relaxed with a newspaper and coffee in an absolute cloud of bed and sheet. They were selling featherbeds and looked intriguingly comfortable. As fast you can say "credit card," I had purchased a featherbed for my husband and me to try out. I put a firm mattress underneath to provide support, with the featherbed on top. When we both flopped onto my concoction, the featherbed embraced us like a marshmallow cloud. Cozy, warm, and playfully fluffy. It made being in bed almost too comfy. The following morning, we felt as happy as the couple in the ad looked. Convinced, I then bought featherbeds for every bed in the house, as well as down comforters to top them. We love them. So do our guests.

Recipe for a Heavenly Bed

Featherbeds are more work to maintain, but they are worth it. You will need:

1 down or down and duck-feather bed
1 featherbed cover
1 down comforter (weights vary)
2 flat sheets
2 fitted sheets
Down pillows with protectors and coverings

Cover your regular mattress (the one on top of the box springs) with the first fitted sheet.

Insert your featherbed inside the cover, zip, and give it a good shake. Then cover the covered featherbed with the fitted sheet (do not include the mattress). This step takes some practice.

Adjust and smooth the excess at the bottom of the bed. The sheet will be looser on the featherbed than it would be on a regular mattress. (I sometimes use an old-country trick.

Take a pole handle from a mop or similar and draw it down the length of the featherbed. It smoothes the featherbed out.) Then put on one flat sheet, leaving about six inches of extra length at the top. Next the down comforter, leaving the six inches loose at the top.

Put on the second flat sheet with the extra six inches at the top.

Take the extra length on the top sheet and double it

under the comforter.

Take the extra sheet length from the sheet under the comforter and fold it over both the comforter and the top sheet. It encloses the comforter in an envelope. Expensive hotels call it double sheeting.

A final topping on the bed can be a quilt or a light covering with pillows and bolsters. Every day the featherbed is used, it must be shaken repeatedly to restore loft. I count 10 shakes for each corner of the featherbed and count it as morning aerobics!

Why would you go to all this trouble? Delayed gratification. One guest said that when she got into the bed, it was like the "best and worst" of times. It was the best bed she had ever slept in and the worst to have to leave!

CHAPTER 7

The Silly Persons Club

Every once in awhile, I drive to Seward, Alaska for a little rest and relaxation at a bed and breakfast perched at the edge of the ocean. I go for the view and the mind-massaging sounds of the waves, not for the breakfast. You have to bring your own snacks. On the entryway table is a guide that informs guests that their breakfast is "in the refrigerator."

A guest should be able to lie in bed and smell something hot and breakfasty, like bacon and eggs with warm aromas swirling up through your waking moments and whispering to your tender morning psyche, "You're on vacation!"

To be fair, my seaside hostess has to go to work in the morning, which is too bad, because she's missing the sound of guests enjoying their morning together at the breakfast table.

It's like cooking a great omelet. The ingredients are a good night's sleep, the smell of breakfast cooking, and a table full of hungry guests. Take a New York stockbroker, a doctor from Berlin, a mountain climber, and a middle-aged couple from Wisconsin. Stir gently. They will froth easily. They're on vacation.

When the guests have been introduced and seated, I serve breakfast, asking questions and filling in with remarks to prime the pump. Where have you been? Where are you going? Do you have pets, children, grandchildren? Did you notice your T-shirt is inside out and backward?

Seated at the breakfast table one morning were one of my favorite couples. They were regulars, here to visit their grandchildren. Danny was a diminutive Irish Catholic from Wisconsin who loved to tell stories. His stories were fun to listen to, earthy and full of Irish brogue.

I liked Danny's fatherly manner toward me. He'd give me a quick shoulder hug and run his hand over my red hair. "Where'd you get those fancy feathers, girly-girl?" he'd ask.

"Hey, Danny, I once heard my grandma talk about the

potato famine. I think maybe I'm one-quarter Irish. What do you think of that?" I said.

"Young lady," Danny twinkled, "I think it's not nice to boast!"

Danny loved to tell stories. He had an earthy tale or a corny joke slipped up his sleeve like a card trick ready to be flashed at the prompt.

"Ready for breakfast, Danny?" I'd ask.

"Breakfast?" Danny flashed. Did I ever tell you the one about the joke book that was being passed around by the prison inmates at breakfast?"

And he'd be off.

His handsome wife, Martha, was a warm, quiet person. The first time I met Martha, she presented me with a hug and a giant wheel of cheddar cheese. Hugs I was familiar with, but I'd never seen that much cheese in one piece. Martha's generosity included listening patiently to Danny's jokes, which could go on a bit.

On this particular morning, guests seated for breakfast, Danny, with his usual early-morning cheer, pulled me close to him, clapped his hand on my shoulder, and looked me in the eye.

He was about to give me some advice. Oh, no, I thought. Experience led me to know I was in for it.

"Sherry," Danny began, "I have three bits of advice to lead you on to a long, enjoyable life."

"Well, gee, thanks, Danny," I replied.

"First of all, Sherry, work hard. I've seen you do it, lass."

"Second, love the Lord. Keep goin' to church as you do." I nodded.

"And third and most importantly, dearie, KEEP THE BOWELS FREE!"

I had an "omigod" moment. Martha looked pained, but the guests seemed amused by Danny's unsolicited advice about God, work, and the importance of good digestion. I like to think the guests were laughing because his advice was good.

* * *

We were waiting for another guest, Keego, a Japanese chemist. He was in Anchorage to present a workshop at the university. During our conversation, I was vaguely aware of the sound of a shower going on and off in his bathroom. The water would run for a few seconds, then go off for half a minute or so. The quick sprinkle again, then off. I suspected Keego was showering the way he would in Japan, using as little water as possible.

So I was surprised when Keego came out of his room with a towel wrapped around his waist and trotted through the dining room and out the back door to the deck. He was headed for the outdoor hot tub.

A few minutes passed before Keego returned looking damp and giving us all a little bow while saying, "Very nice, very nice." Then we heard the shower start up again. On, off. On, off. Pause. Keego bowed his way through the dining room again en route to the tub. Hot tub, simmer, shower, and repeat. "Very nice." Keego smiled once more as he headed to the shower.

We all smiled and found ourselves bowing in return. We figured he was doing what he would do in Japan. He was so polite and formal, even in a towel.

Finally, he arrived, fully clothed at the breakfast table with a smile and a bowed greeting to all. "Very nice system you have. Very nice." I thought that under his formality I detected a bit of mischief in his eyes.

After I introduced Keego to Martha and Danny, as well as to the other guests, Keego studied the bowl of blueberries in front of him without making a move to eat them.

Looking perplexed, Keego nodded again and then asked politely, "How shall I enjoy this?"

We were all a bit slow on the uptake, not quite understanding the question.

When Keego asked once again, "How shall I enjoy this?" it finally clicked. Ah, bet he's never seen blueberries before. At least not running around loose.

Danny saved the day by demonstrating his best blueberry chasing technique. Spoon in, dramatic flourish to the mouth. I wouldn't know until later that in Japan, it's customary for the guest to wait until the hostess formally offers the dish. Oops.

"Hey, Keego," Danny asked. "Have you ever heard the joke about the pig and the three farmers?"

"Uh, no," Keego replied, "but there's a Japanese version about a pig and a fire."

So they were off telling pig jokes, just two funny guys over coffee, egging each other on. It seemed like every Irish joke had its Japanese clone. Buddies now, Danny and Keego shared anecdotes until everyone else had wandered off. Martha gave up trying to corral Danny for the day. She knew her man; he'd keep Keego there as long as he could. Martha went shopping.

That morning, I went to Keego's room to clean. When I raised the bed pillow to change the cover, I found a surprise: a fresh dollar bill nested in the sheets. "Ah, the sweetie, he left me a tip," I thought. Not appropriate but cute.

Later in the day, I instructed Keego. "It was nice of you to leave me a tip, but in our country, we don't leave a tip under the pillow." He smiled sweetly and nodded.

The next day, while remaking his bed, I found Keego had ignored me. A second dollar was snuggled under the pillow. Obviously, he wasn't paying much attention to my advice.

On Keego's third and last day, neither of us mentioned our cultural confusion. I was becoming quite fond of him and his sneaky dollar bills.

As Keego prepared to leave, He signed our guestbook

with his name and address in beautiful calligraphy. He invited me to visit him in Japan "It snows in Kyoto. I take you skiing."

He stood before me, ready to say goodbye, his arms held captive by his weighty backpack. Although Keego was helpless and I knew hugging was not a Japanese custom, I just couldn't help myself.

Ignoring Keego's shyness, I threw my arms around him and his backpack and hugged him hugely while I planted a goodbye kiss on his cheek. Keego's face flamed red. He gave me a big, slow smile over his shoulder as he stumbled out a little unsteadily.

As the taxi pulled away, I stood on the porch to wave goodbye. I could see his face pressed against the car window for one last peek back at me. He returned my wave and was gone.

When the taxi turned the corner, I raced to his room, tantalized. Would there be a dollar there? I turned over the pillow only to be disappointed. There was no dollar.

I realized, somewhat sadly, that I had Americanized him. Then, right next to the pillow, I saw it. A small preprinted white business card stating, "You are now a member of the Silly Persons Club." When I turned it over, there were happy stick figures with laughing mouths. "You ARE a silly person," it read. He had written my name in the membership blank provided.

Keego, Keego, come back! I am a silly person. I worry too much. No dollar for me. I was laughing. Was he? I was still a little perplexed. Why did I get this card?

I decided to do an Internet search with the words "Japan, silly person." I got half a million references. No help there. Thinking, thinking.

So what if I had tried to explain a Garfield cartoon to Keego. "See, there's this cat with an attitude, hanging on to a backdoor screen, four paws spread out with a terrorized look on his face!" Would Keego laugh at Garfield? He certainly thought Danny was funny.

Although I never got to Kyoto, Keego comes to mind quite often for me, usually in connection with food; more specifically, unfamiliar food. Food like deep-fried shrimp heads, chopped seaweed appetizer, or little chunks of raw fish on rice beds.

Remembering Keego and the bowl of blueberries, I ask myself, "How shall I enjoy this?" I try to ask it when I get up in the morning, before greeting guests or serving them breakfast, or working the guests for a laugh.

As a question, it forms a rather good prayer. "Dear Lord, how shall I enjoy this day?"

Puffy Omelet with Herbs

A puffy omelet with a creamy sauce is just spectacular and tastes light on the tongue. I make sure my guests are half an hour from the table before I begin cooking it. Although the omelet serves four, my husband and I often share it for dinner.

4 eggs
4 tbsp milk or cream
Salt and pepper
2 tbsp soft, finely chopped bread crumbs
Fresh herbs, any mixture chopped
4 tbsp butter
A light white cream sauce with a small amount of cheese added (optional)

Soak bread crumbs in milk
Separate egg whites from yolks.
Beat egg whites in large bowl until stiff.
Beat yolks in bowl until creamy.
Stir in milk, salt and pepper.
Add chopped herbs to yolk mixture. Reserve some herbs for garnish.
Fold into egg whites.
Turn into a skillet of sizzling butter (I recommend a nonstick pan).
Turn heat to low and cook eggs slowly.
Cook omelet gently until light brown underneath.

Transfer to a 350 oven. Bake until set on top (about 15 minutes).

Roll omelet onto hot platter, folding as you roll.

Pour a small amount of cheese sauce over omelet (optional) and garnish with sprigs of fresh herbs.

Serves four.

CHAPTER 8

Sky Kings

Tundra hopping in a warm

DeHavilland Beaver above

Bears and blueberries,

Game birds and mosquitoes,

Fish running

Varied rainbow,

Speckled glory,

Through hard running rivers,

I know as we fly,

It is memory.

—Sherry Tomlinson—

The problem with getting into the country in Alaska is that most of it is off the road system. To enjoy the wilderness experience, travelers and residents alike get into light airplanes on their way to fun. Tales of near misses, misses, poor runways, bad weather, and bad judgments abound.

Recently my husband and I were invited to fly along with some guests to dig for razor clams. We made the one-hour hop to a beach across Cook Inlet in their small-wheeled plane against a buffeting wind.

In spite of the wind pounding our faces and a large, unleashed Lab running in circles waking up the clams, we dug our limit, ate a sandy snack on the beach, and joined in a gut-popping shove to get the plane out of soft sand with the incoming tide lapping at our heels. We were back for lunch in Anchorage by noon. Time for a nap.

I recall a fishing adventure when it took eight hours of multiple round trips in a tiny Piper J3 Cub to ferry my husband and me, a dog, and enough gear for a weekend fishing trip. Tony, the pilot of the mothlike plane, was both a friend and a guest. At Summit Lake, according to Department of Fish and Game regulations, the minimum length of a trout taken had to be twenty-four inches. Think of that! Twenty-four inches minimum length. A fishermen's dream!

Tony and my husband vibrated like a fish rubbing the lure when they talked about it. They found out many fishing hours later that nearly every rainbow in Summit Lake, at least the ones they were catching, was twenty-three inches. Maximum.

On our second day, the two men flew down to the other end of the lake to search for fish big enough to keep. I stayed in camp with Murphy, our sixty-five-pound springer spaniel. Murphy was supposed to protect me. You know, bark when there is something large and alive in the area.

I was enjoying my lakeside aloneness, watching the twenty-inch speckled trout swim by in the shallows, when Tony taxied up in the J3, leaned out the cockpit window, and yelled: "Get in, NOW! There are bears just up shore from you."

I got in and sat in the second seat as Tony hefted Murphy into the tail section. He powered up the plane as he began his taxi down to the other end of the long lake. I was holding my breath as he increased his speed, revving up through those tense moments between earth and sky. Finally, the plane started to rise and roar. I had just started to breathe out when there was a huge whump. The floats slammed back down onto the water's surface.

Tony yelled into my microphone as we hit hard, "I couldn't get it up cause of ol' big butt back there!"

"Thanks a lot, asshole!" I screamed.

"Not you," he said, laughing. "Murphy!"

You can still see pictures of us all on that trip at a local burger joint. The owner posts pictures of Alaskans who have been patrons over the years. Next to the smiling people in the photos, there is usually a dead fish or an airplane. In ours, there are both. I'm smiling for the camera because I'm thinking: "Whoopee! I'm still alive!"

* * *

Many of us have to fly when we want to see our relatives. My in-laws live on a narrow finger of land that points away from the fishing village of Seldovia, toward the city of Homer. To get there in summer, we make a five-hour drive from Anchorage; a one-hour boat trip across Kachemak Bay, weather permitting; and then offload into a smaller, shallower skiff to reach the dock and home. In winter, we make the fifteen-minute hop across the bay in a light plane.

The first time I flew to Seldovia, Alaska was in a six-passenger Cessna. Our pilot, Harry, was cranky and our only choice. There is a tale told about Harry. Supposedly a cat got loose and crazy in the cockpit of the Cessna. Harry managed to grab the cat and, without so much as a "with your permission" to the owner, opened the window and pitched the cat out. Real moody guy.

As we flew across Kachemak Bay, big gray clouds dominated the sky above, and nasty white-crested waves argued below. The fishing boats had already been tucked into the harbor. The lurching began at takeoff.

Terrified and airsick, I closed my eyes and mind and took a vacation from my body. I was now tucked between the wings of a giant white swan. The plane's drops, bumps, and creaking were transformed into the natural playfulness of my beautiful bird in flight.

Through the fog of my visualization, I could hear my husband's voice pointing out landmarks below: "There's Gull Rock on the left, Yukon Island, Peterson Cove, and Little Tutka Lagoon. But I was with Happy Gilmore, in a happier place.

When we were finally on the ground again, my husband said apologetically: "Oh, honey, when I looked over at you, your face was green. I'm so sorry. I had no idea you were afraid."

Well, while I had to get over it if I wanted to see relatives and spend time in a place so beautiful it could be called Paradise, I've never learned to love the hop across the bay.

Once, when we had scheduled a morning flight, I awoke to the roar of the ocean waves pounding on the gabions outside our bedroom window. There was a nasty wind shaking the boards of the house. Surely the flight would be canceled.

As we unloaded baggage and dogs onto the tarmac, I prayed, "Please, Harry, don't show up." But I could see his plane banking over the tree-covered mountains that ring the short strip, wheels hitting the ice-covered runway as he rolled out to a stop.

Harry got out of the plane without so much as a hello. We all stood there waiting for him to speak. Finally, he barked: "Well, are you flying or not? Load it up!"

My husband sat in the back of the plane with the dogs. They were soon asleep with the lulling sound of the engine. I sat in the front seat with two passengers behind me. "Pull your seat belts tight," yelled Harry. "Get ready to rock and roll!"

We did that, all right. The flight was brutal, nasty, and short. When we stumbled out of the plane, the passenger who sat behind me apologized profusely. "I'm so sorry."

She had thrown up in the hood of my parka.

* * *

I'm sitting in a floatplane this morning, holding my arms close to my body to protect myself from the early-morning chill. We slowly circle the lakeshore while the oil heats up to the temperature that will allow us to begin our take-off run over the waters of Iliamna Lake. It could rightly be called the Sea of Iliamna for its oceanic size.

My thoughts rise with the pale September sun, and I think about dying. Flying and death are two words that seem to go together in Alaska. The weather, mountains, overloaded planes, and cocky pilots make flying danger-ous. Anyone who has lived here for a while has received a phone call informing him that a friend's or relative's air-craft has crashed into ground, water, or mountainside. The grief goes with the place.

I'm not phobic anymore. You just can't stay scared all the time. And in a place like Alaska, who wants to stay at home? Not me. Today I'll fly in the seat next to an experienced pilot, lodge owner, and good friend.

We will be flying over autumnal tundra reddened by blueberry bushes. There will be sparse yellow willows and fish-filled rivers. Although we'll see some bears and a few caribou, we'll fly for hours without seeing another human being. The plane makes my friend a monarch in his kingdom. Because he has access, this land and its beauty are his, and for today only, I'm royalty.

Along with my husband, two of our springer spaniel hunting dogs, Basil and Sadie-Blux, are seated in the back of the Beaver floatplane along with my new 28-gauge shotgun. The shotgun is a lightweight field gun. I've already put thousands of shells through the barrel at the local shooting range. My friends teasingly call me Annie Oakley. But in spite of my accuracy on the range, I've never brought down a bird. I've been hunting several times already this fall, but I keep missing.

Because we are a family with a hunting tradition, I have no problem with shooting supper. But there is the fact that I keep shooting late—or "behind the bird," as they say.

Our pilot and good friend, a lodge owner at Lake Iliamna, has announced wryly that his 12-year-old nephew had no trouble hitting a bird last weekend. The pressure is on.

After landing at a small lake, we start our walk over the soggy tundra muskeg. It's like walking over a wet mattress, in boots. We encounter flocks ranging over the hillocks before scattering into the scrubby willow. The men shoot a couple of birds and then move on without decimating the flock. I'm still shooting late.

After the first few miles, I forget my fear of hat hair and welcome a mosquito head net. I'm able to breathe again without sucking mosquitoes up my nose. At least five miles later, the shotgun has become my cross. I'm sweating in my head net when a ptarmigan flies up in front of me.

"It's yours!" my husband cries. I have to shoot. It's an easy crossing-shot.

I mount my gun and fire. The ptarmigan falls in a flurry of wings. Upon command, Basil retrieves the still form and brings it to my hand. "Good boy, Basil," I say as I hold the still-warm bird. My husband is so excited. "Let's get a picture. It's your first bird!"

I have that picture still. In spite of the wan smile I'm wearing, I have a rugged, "I am woman" look with shotgun in hand and Basil next to me holding the ptarmigan in his mouth.

"Aren't you proud?" beams my husband.

"Not really," I reply, giving Basil a rub. "Shooting a bird was like losing my virginity. I'm just relieved it's over."

When the rest of the hunting party comes over to congratulate me, Derek is on his back in the tundra, laughing. He has to tell everyone what I just said.

I suppose my ribaldry was funny to everyone else, but I wasn't trying to be clever. I'm pretty certain that I'll never be a virgin or shoot a bird again.

CHAPTER 9

A Parisian in Anchorage

"Bon jour," said the good-looking, rangy Frenchman in wonderfully accented English as he monkey-climbed into our large American SUV. It was his first trip to the United States. He was leaving the most expensive hotel in town to spend time in our little bed and breakfast. An Air France employee with a long weekend in Anchorage, Rene wanted to stay someplace a little cozier. When I picked him up, it was a zero-degree February day, the coldest time of winter.

Anchorage was in full winter dress with trees and lampposts, rooftops, and the statue of Captain Cook all heavily mantled in snow. As we drove through town, we could see over the snow banked on both sides of the street across to Cook Inlet and the Chugach Mountains. A blue water-colored sky feathered into the rise of Mount Susitna, a mountain locals call Sleeping Lady for her recumbent posture as she faces Anchorage.

As Rene and I looked back at the Lady, he gave his note of approval, a click of the tongue. I was to learn that when Rene became happy or elated, he had a novel habit. He would give a little click, not a chickenlike cluck or a disapproving "tsk-tsk" sound but a sharp little explosion of tongue against palate. A click. I didn't know if it was a French custom or just Rene, but I thought it was charming.

Rene never rented a car, so his daily routine was to walk the several miles to town and back on Anchorage's urban coastal trail. He wore a red plaid wool coat in the near-zero temperatures. He declined the offer of something warmer. Where does one buy a hunter-type coat in stylish Paris, I wondered.

After we returned home from our workday, Rene would show up from his walk with a red, chapped face. I suspected he was the only one down there on the trails being slapped in the face by the northern wind.

"How was your day?" I'd ask, feeling a little guilty that I couldn't take him sightseeing.

"Fantastique!" Then the happy little click. Rene was a

quiet guy. I can imagine his day was similar to mine when I wander on a rainy day in Paris: stores, galleries, cups of expensive coffee, people-watching.

Rene was delighted when my husband volunteered to take him ice fishing, Alaska style. That involved an air mattress, sleeping bags for comfort on the ice and a bottle of brandy to kill the pain.

I have a somewhat cynical view of men at play. Some guys like to go off with a buddy on "adventures" and do unwise things that get them into trouble. Then they'll have a story to tell other guys. Women can only spoil the fun with the truth. In fact, when a woman is invited along on a trip, I suspect her man picks the nastiest day and the roughest trails with the deepest mud holes and most impenetrable woods, all of which will make her so miserable that she will never want to go again.

I know for a fact that when one friend's son joined a hunting trip, my husband advised him: "Tell your mother it was rainy, cold, and wet, that you were miserable and the only good thing all day was the yummy lunch she packed for you."

When it comes to hunting and fishing, the truth is not in them.

Back to the ice fishing. Once they were there with their supplies, I think the fishing went pretty well, and when the brandy couldn't keep them warm anymore, it was time to go home. So everything—fishing gear, guns and ammo, and extra cold-weather gear—was bungeed onto a sled.

The beauty of my husband's grand plan was that the sled dogs would do all the work. However, somewhere someone lost control of the dogs who then careened off into the deep snow with harnesses flying everywhere. The bungee cords broke loose. There was a wild free-for-all of alcohol-challenged men chasing dogs through the trees. Finally, the dogs were retrieved. Boys, boys!

I figure they lost nearly $1,000 worth of gear that day, including a gun. I never did learn where my husband got the black eye. By the time they got home, the men were pretty quiet about the whole affair.

The two of them, however, had proof of their fishing prowess. Rene and my husband proudly dumped a fresh trout into the kitchen sink. The trout was at least 20 inches long and its rainbow glistened through a coat of ice.

I suspect that a Paris art gallery, however grand, could never yield any object more beautiful to Rene than that fish. Rene studied it, his eyes dancing. "Will you stuff the fish with grass?"

My husband and I exchanged glances. Marijuana-stuffed fish? Ohhhhh, he means herbs. So stuffed with grass it was. Rene shared our dinner of fresh trout, rice, and salad. The food was exquisite. After wine, the company was exhausted but content.

Rene now had one afternoon left in Anchorage. Although I was tired from my workday, I offered to take Rene for a drive. Twenty minutes from the bed and breakfast is Chugach State Park, with half a million acres of mountainous wilderness. In summer, the park is full of berries, berry pickers, and berry-eating bears. Hiking trails wind through wildflower-filled meadows, streams pitching sharply downward, and small blue glacial lakes that, if you climb high enough, give way to scree-covered, knife-narrow ridges.

As I negotiated the steep hairpin turns that led up to the park entrance, the world turned pink with alpenglow. In an Alaska winter, at a certain time of the day, the cold air literally turns the mountains, the sky, and the very fingers in front of your frozen nose a true rosy lavender color.

Below us, Fire Island was nestled in the ice floes of Cook Inlet. The wide expanse of the Alaska Range popped out in front of us. Sleeping Lady reclined in the receding sunset. Rene's happy clicks become more rhythmic as we drove slowly up the mountain's curvaceous side.

Once parked, we climbed up to the visitors' platform; the six hours of light the winter had granted us was already fading. Standing there, we could see 360 degrees of snowy mountains, turning hot colors in the escaping light. The wind swirled around us as we slowly turned in a circle and tried to take it in.

The first time I saw a painting by the Alaskan artist Fred Machetanz, with winter landscapes painted in purple-blues and glowing pinks, my mind said, "Naw, not possible." But a late-evening sunset in cold, rarified air can have, in fact, a fake-looking fluorescence much like the scene Rene and I were seeing below. A snowy world in Technicolor. Machetanz got it right.

The stars began to show themselves in the darkening sky. We gasped with the cold, then ran for the car.

The weekend over, Rene was saying his goodbyes. With guests, I always pretend our paths will cross again. It is an emotionally convenient ritual. "How lucky you are to live in Paris," I said. And meant it.

"But, no, Cherrie. Paris is just a big city like any other," Rene said.

So while I may dream of a pretty stucco house in a sun-drenched French Provencal village, I suspect that maybe Rene dreams of Anchorage. Perhaps he remembers the rainbow stripe on a trout fresh from a wilderness lake. Or meeting new friends in an American city. Or the pink veil of alpenglow on snowy mountains. Maybe he remembers a huge, wild land inhabited with so few people.

Or is it possible that after some good French wine, he expands a bit and tells his wife: "Anchorage was bitter, cold, and lonely, just a big, empty place. Really, my dear, the only pleasant part of the trip was your daily phone call." Click.

CHAPTER 10

Airplane Man

Bush planes get Alaskans out there in a land so big some pilots call Alaska "The Big Empty." It's not really, of course. We fly when we want to do business, lobby at the state capital in Juneau, or visit far-flung relatives and friends. But it's the desire to see wildlife that gets most of us on the plane. Like my friend Angie.

Angie is one of our favorite bed and breakfast guests, a businesswoman from the Northwest. She was introduced to bush flying by a man she met on her flight from Seattle. He was a pilot who owned his own air taxi service, they hit it off, why not show the little lady some of the country? She called her volunteer pilot "Airplane Man."

Let me tell you a bit about Angie. For starters, her name fits. Angie looks like an angel. She once said, "Men like me." She seemed amazed by that. I had to explain it to her.

"You have blond hair, big baby blues, Jolie-like lips, and a drop-dead body. Duh!" Angie's also funny and smart, and she remembers the details of my life better than I do.

It didn't take long before Angie's new acquaintance made good on his offer. He needed to fly a client to a lodge north of Anchorage. They could look for wildlife, see some country. Angie was thrilled to be invited. So early the next morning, Airplane Man and Angie headed off to see wild things from the air. Angie had her camera ready for a bear.

I should explain that bear sightings are rare unless you're near their food sources: berries in the fall or a lake or stream full of salmon. It takes a big territory to provide enough food for a large animal like a bear to survive through a long winter. For a bear, fatter is better.

Angie and her friend had an hour or so of good flying after they dropped their passenger off at the lodge and headed home. They had a chance to skim over the tundra; moose were browsing the willows. As they started through the pass, the flying weather turned bad. Dark clouds obscured the narrows between the mountains ahead; the wind started bumping the plane.

Angie was wearing earphones to protect her ears from the engine noise. There was a microphone attached to the phones so the pilot and passenger could talk to each other. As the plane's nose wheel came up, so did Angie's anxiety. Airplane Man mouthed into his microphone, "Hold on, Angie, we've got a little weather here."

It was a rowdy dance the plane was doing when Angie's stomach started to pitch with the plane. That didn't stop her from protesting continuously into the mike. "Omigod. Omigod." Her "omigods" got louder until her friend pointed at his mike. "For the love of God, PLEASE SHUT UP!"

Threading the Beaver under the cloud cover and keeping altitude was not as big a problem at this point as Angie was.

"We're going to die!" Angie screamed into her microphone as the plane dipped and twisted and roared. "We're going to die! We're going to die!"

Airplane Man looked wildly over and ripped off his earphones. He was about to experience death by decibel level.

"Put me down. Put me down—NOW!"

Airplane Man did just that. The plane rocked down under the clouds, to a small lake with a lather of waves across its face. To manage the wind, he came down full throttle, and just as they dropped to the surface, he cut the power as a wall of water rose in front of them. They were definitely down.

Throwing an ugly glance his way, Angie looked around. On the shoreline there was a small cabin with a skiff tied to a rough dock. It might have looked picturesque if it weren't for the group of bears fishing on the bank outside the cabin door.

"OK, little missy. There you go," Airplane Man drawled softly. "I can put you ashore. I'll call the Coast Guard to come and get you when the weather clears. It shouldn't take more than a couple of days for them to get here."

Angie studied the bears on the beach. They looked like they owned the place.

"Or," her friend continued, "you can go back up with me and take your chances."

Let's see, Airplane Man or the bears. Angie gave her

answer in a very small voice: "OK, I'll go back with you, I guess."

"And don't put on that microphone!" he yelled as he revved the engine to begin the wild spiral around the lake that would give them the speed they needed to step up on the water and fly.

Angie not only made it back safely, but she was to become a bear-watching fanatic. Throughout the years she stayed with us, she always made time to go to Katmai National Park to see what her furry friends were doing.

One evening I was shocked to see Angie on the six–o'clock news. A video clip showed Angie holding her ground while a blackie charged her. Halfway through his assault, the bear halted, turned around, and snorted off. He knew when to back off!

Angie hadn't even mentioned her encounter with the bear. I wondered if Airplane Man had given Angie, the experienced bear watcher, the choice again—to stay in the cabin with the bear family or fly back into the storm—which she would chose.

She never really had to worry about Airplane Man, you

know. There's a threadbare Alaska truism: "There are old pilots and bold pilots, but no old, bold pilots." Airplane Man was old enough to know how to fly and bold enough to offer a pretty lady a ride.

Sherry's Creamy Quiche

This moist quiche is featured in an online bed and breakfast cookbook. If you slice a small tomato, such as a Roma, and arrange the slices over the top before baking, it will add cheery color to a bubbling-hot quiche.

Pastry for one-crust pie (In a pinch, you can skip the crust—just spray muffin cups well before arranging your fillings in the cups).

> *1 cup smoked salmon or other seafood*
> *Sub: cooked sausage, ham, mushrooms, sautéed veggies*
> *4 ounces cheese*
> *Sub: cheddar or Mexican mixture*
> *1/2 cup mayonnaise (not lite)*
> *4 eggs*
> *1 cup milk (or half and half)*
> *Herbs to taste (fresh are great)*
> *Salt and pepper*

Line pie plate with crust.
Fill with cheese, meat, or veggie mixture and herbs.
Beat remaining ingredients.
Pour over filling.
Bake at 350 for about 40 minutes, until lightly browned and set in the center.

Serves four to six.

CHAPTER 11

Boot Camp B&B

Burnout is high among bed and breakfast hosts. It's hard work that you've taken home with you. When my energy is playing out, I do the sensible thing. Call my mommy.

"Are you coming up to see us this summer, Mom?"

"I don't know, honey. I'm not sure I can survive another one of your fishing trips. Last year when we went fishing, I almost fell into the Kenai River."

"Mom, I'm not taking you fishing. Let's go for a little no-stress ferry trip. Blue water, glaciers, wildlife, lots of wildflowers. Honest to goodness, Mom, Prince William Sound is the doggone eighth wonder of the world. I'll buy you an ice cream cone. You'll love it. How about it?"

"I don't know. Every time I come, I get cold and wet."

"Mom, I promise you sunshine."

So Mom and I were set. We'd take a ferry ride on Prince

William Sound to the port town of Valdez and stay at a bed and breakfast. B&Bs are more fun. I learn by being a guest in other bed and breakfasts.

Often I see genuine hospitality. Last winter a hostess was saying goodbye to her guest. It was cold outside. As the guest stood at the door, the hostess reached up and gently adjusted the wool scarf around his neck and tucked it in close to him. It was such a small gesture, but it told her guest how very welcome he was in her home.

Soon, Mom and I were off to see the sea with dripping ice cream cones in our hands. It's easy to come by a cone in Alaska. We are the nation's highest per-capita consumers of ice cream. Go figure. We bought them at a little sweet shop near the ferry dock. Mom had double fudge chocolate. Pistachio for me. When we walked across the ferry gangplank to the passenger solarium, I was Mom's favorite daughter.

Oh, happy day, the sun was shining. We sat deck-side with a backpack full of snacks. Although we were in the cheap seats, we had a first-class view of Prince William Sound.

We were surrounded by mountains with creamy tops. The slopes were like pictures of Ireland, oh so green. Deep fjords cut back through the mountainsides, and frothing water was falling out over rocks like a bridal veil.

We could see icebergs in the water, floating offshore. Columbia Glacier glistened in the distance. A visiting auntie once asked about the glacial ice, "How do they get it so blue, dear?" I don't know if she thought there might be a small plane that flies over with a batch of blue dye to dump, just to make it pretty, or what.

I respectfully explained: "Well, Auntie, this is what I think happens. The glacier has gathered snow and ice for millions of years. The weight of all that ice is tremendous. Over time, it compresses, gets sort of elasticity, and turns blue-looking." Miss Science, that's me.

Our ferry pilot drew closer to the looming glacier. Mom and I held hands and gave each other "oh, goody" looks. As the pilot gave off a few loud blasts of the ferry's horn, the sound vibrations sent skyscraper-sized shards of ice calving off the Columbia. There was a thunderous crash as tons of ancient ice hit the water with a giant slosh.

121

And then, as my mother remembers, the pilot turned off the engines and we sat. The pilot didn't shout to us over his microphone, "Let's take a minute and everyone stop talking." But people did get quiet, as if we were in a cathedral. And then, at the edge of that ancient ice field, there was perfect silence.

Toward evening, we were able to take off our sweaters. Here we were, on the deck of the ferry at nine o'clock in the evening, the sun shining like it was high noon, surrounded by enough ice to keep Mexico in margaritas for the millennium, and still warm enough to wear shirtsleeves.

We ate salami sandwiches and sipped bourbon out of a sack while all sorts of ducks ducked and scooted around us. Little tropical-colored puffins were as visible as a fisherman's bobber popping up and down in the water.

Sea lions and seals were stretched out on ice floes. Mom said: "Gosh, honey, they're stretched out like bathing beauties posing on the ice. They don't look cold at all."

Next to the ferry, sea otter families munched on mollusks. When a killer whale swam at the stern of the boat, as if hoping for a fishy handout, people with video cameras jostled at the rail.

The pilot slowed and stopped once again so we could watch the whales. They were cavorting around the ferry, actually swimming under the boat before bursting out the other side. They made eye contact as they circled and surfaced. I felt a brief, happy insanity. I wanted to laugh and cry at the same time

As Mom and I gripped each other's hands in excitement, there was a flip of a fin and the whales were gone.

"What more could we ask for?" Mom said.

"For the captains of oil tankers to stay sober," I said. "It's taken years for this place to get rid of the gunk of the Exxon Valdez."

I quoted an ex-governor of Alaska: "You just can't let nature run wild." In Prince William Sound, thank goodness, once again nature was completely out of hand.

Mom and I were flush with good weather, Prince William's regal Sound, and the contents of the paper sack as we disembarked at Valdez. After a short walk, we arrived at our B&B pulling our wheely suitcases behind us. Still a bit giddy, we rang the doorbell.

"Where have you been?" Our hostess glowered. "It's almost eleven o'clock." She was in her bathrobe, and she looked tired. Uh-oh.

"The ferry just got in," I explained. "So sorry."

As we entered the foyer, we saw the first sign, a five-by-eight card that commanded us in bold letters, "DO NOT walk into this house with your shoes on." We did as we were told. We took our shoes off.

I looked around as we were led downstairs to our room. Lots of knickknacks everywhere invitingly perched to be bumped and broken. Dried bouquets of flowers were tucked in here and there. Potpourri-scent cloyed in our noses after the day's ocean air. There was a lot of pink.

As we were led to our quarters, we noticed more DO NOT messages along the way. Signs were scattered among the fussy pillows and tacked on walls. Paper warnings were everywhere. DO NOT leave lights on when leaving the room.

We were busy reading signs when our hostess asked us, "Would you like breakfast at the seven, eight, or nine o'clock seating in the morning?"

Mother and I looked at each other and hesitated. Our tiny hostess seemed to fluff up like a little ticked-off bird that might give peck one of us if we made the wrong move. Somehow I felt guilty when she looked at me. I definitely got the feeling that I was in her house.

"I would prefer you came at eight," our hostess asserted.

"Sure," we replied together like two obedient children.

A white card greeted us as we walked in. DO NOT eat in the room. Mom looked at the sign and worried. "We better not be late for breakfast or we'll get into trouble. I'll set the alarm clock."

"Mom, you know we'll both have to get up in the middle of the night to go to the bathroom. By the way, where is the bathroom?"

"Down the hall, sweetie." Oh, boy.

I was looking at the bed covered with pink satin pillows when I read DO NOT put luggage on the bed. Made sense to me.

When the buzzer went off in the morning, Mom jumped out of bed, bopped out the bedroom door in her jammies, headed for the bathroom for a shower, and was back within minutes.

Big problem. There was only one bathroom for four bedrooms. Currently, that one bathroom was occupied by two teenagers who were braiding each other's hair. Any parent knows that two teenagers plus one bathroom equals no bathroom. Mother got more and more tense, pacing our room. She had two problems: we were late for breakfast, and she still had to go.

There was a sharp rap on the door. Mom jumped. It was our hostess. She wasn't looking very friendly when she announced, "Your breakfast is ready." She turned and walked away.

My poor unwashed and unrelieved mother panicked. "What'll we do, sweetheart? Our breakfast is ready!"

"Mom, get a grip. This is not boot camp; this is called vacation." Just then we saw another note:

FIVE-MINUTE LIMIT IN THE BATHROOM

Remember

Other Guests are Waiting

We held each other's eyes and then collapsed on the frilly bed in hysterics. And when you have to pee real bad, that's not funny!

"The Do Not boot camp," we repeated, gasping. We were having fun, at last. And, gratefully, it wasn't long before the girls had their hair right and Mom got her five minutes in the bathroom.

When we sat down at 8:30, breakfast looked pretty meager. A serving plate held a small amount of scrambled eggs. The guests politely took small servings to go with their plain white toast. No juice or fruit. Some limp bacon on a plate. Pointing to a lonely bowl of jam, our hostess said, "Strawberry jam is good on toast." I was embarrassed for her.

Suddenly, without warning, I had to go. NOW. I knew the downstairs bathroom was taken, and I couldn't wait. Taking the hostess aside, I pleaded: "Please, do you have another bathroom I can use? It's an emergency."

Grudgingly, she led me to her bedroom-bath suite. Once in the bathroom, instead of DO NOT signs, I saw framed pictures on the wall. Our hostess had once been in show business. She was posing in various costumes, and they all showed a lot of leg. Wow, she had been a knockout!

Maybe running a bed and breakfast was a long way from the footlights. Maybe she'd had better days than this one. And although I felt a bit more sympathetic seeing her in her glory days, I couldn't imagine her tenderly adjusting my neck scarf so I'd be warm on a cold night.

We dusted our feet as we left the Boot Camp Bed and breakfast. We couldn't get out of there fast enough. As we stood waiting for our short airplane hop home, Mom silently formed the O's in DO NOT with big rounded lips. We giggled like girls. I felt like Ethel Mertz in an old "I Love Lucy" episode. Mom and I still cannot say DO NOT to each other without laughing. It would never happen at the Hilton. Not the notes, not the hostess. Definitely not the fun.

Yummy Fruit Parfait

Guests' eyes widen when fruit parfait is presented in beautiful goblet. Layer the following just before serving.

Bananas, orange chunks, apple, fresh berries, any well-drained fruit
Yogurt—vanilla, peach or blueberry

Sprinkle nutty granola on top.
Garnish with a berry and sprig of fresh mint if you have it.

CHAPTER 12

Making Memories in McCarthy

Bed and breakfasts can be charmingly quirky anywhere, but in Alaska, staying in bed and breakfast lodging
can get downright adventurous. Your hostess might show
you to a nook-sized bedroom in a Quonset hut or an op-
ulent suite in a hillside mansion, complete with fitness
center. The bathroom can be outdoors or have no doors.
Worse-case scenario: outdoors with no doors!

Hoping for an adventure, my husband and I chose to
stay in a bed and breakfast for our honeymoon trip to Mc-
Carthy, Alaska. We'd never been to the remote town in the
Interior region. After a day's drive from Anchorage, there
is more than sixty miles of rough gravel road. Driving on
gravel doesn't bother me; Alaska is full of bumpy roads.
What I dreaded was the bridge we'd have to cross to get to
McCarthy.

After a long, dusty drive, there it was. The bridge was one lane with no retaining walls, not even a guardrail. To cross it, we bumped our tires onto the two flat wooden rails that served as the floor. Our continued existence depended on my husband's ability to drive straight. I knew that on this little puppy, there were no U-turns allowed.

As we started across, I could see the blue sky above and the river beneath. This might be the scenic route, but I didn't want to look. In an old cheesy movie, "Sheena of the Jungle," the heroine is about to be ravaged by the bad guy when her helpless father shouts, "Leave your body, Sheena!" For a moment, I became Sheena and left my body.

Finally we were bumping off the bridge, safe on the other side, though we'd have to do it again on the return trip.

The final obstacle on the road was crossing the Kennecott River in a hand-pulled tram. Before 1997, the tram was the only way to cross the Kennecott River into McCarthy. Today you can take a footbridge to the other side, but you still can't drive across.

At that time, however, you had to get into a bucket seat attached to a pulley. It ran on a cable across the river.

Once the seat was launched, it made a screaming swoosh down the line. You had to trust the person you were with to pull you across the river. If you'd been naughty, your partner could leave you dangling until you turned nice.

I avoided looking down at the grey, glacier fed river galloping below me as my husband helped me into the tram seat. He was about to cast me off down the line when, at the last second, he reached up and snatched my heavy braid out of the cable. My hair had become entangled in the gear. I was a nanosecond away from being scalped, the hard way.

Before I could sense relief, I was swinging down the cable toward the riverbed and up again to land safely on the opposite bank. When someone mentions McCarthy, I still scratch my noggin a bit.

The big sag I had just survived on the cable would be the first of two I would experience that day. The second would be in our bed. Both had their share of danger.

After a short backpack into town, we located our bed and breakfast, a historic old mill that had been converted into lodging. It was surrounded by cathedral like mountains.

There was a wild river running behind the millworks.

Our hostess escorted us up rickety stairs to our room. That's when we got our first look at our nighttime nemesis. When you visit a historic site, you don't want it to be your bed. We could see springs looking completely sprung underneath. When we jumped on the bed to test it out, it threw us on top of each other. It was wrestlemania just to maintain position. It was the bed from hell.

That night, in our honeymoon bed, I discovered that when it comes to sleep, my new husband was a ferocious infighter. He slept in the middle of the bed most of the night, where everything rolled, eventually.

In the morning, I tried to ignore nature's call as long as I could. I wasn't feeling too nimble after a night in the roller-coaster bed. In order to make my move, I released a primal scream to get my adrenalin going, did a sort of leaping dismount out of the bed, threw on yesterday's clothes, and headed out the window. Yeah, that's how a guest got to the toilet. Go through a window, climb a ladder down the outside of the house, and take a little hike. Over the river, through the woods, etc. In spite of dive-bombing mosquitoes en route to the bathroom, I made it. Ever try to squat while slapping mosquitoes? I was a lot younger then.

For a shower, the hostess showed us a traditional outdoor banya. Inside the wooden structure were buckets of water, an old-fashioned black woodstove for heating water in long-handled pans, and willow switches.

Banya bathing requires teamwork; it's very social. The method goes like this. You and your partner sit in a very hot room with wooden grates on the floor. You get nice and warm and when your pores say hello, you soap up and ladle water over each other with the pans of warm water. Then you switch each other gently with the willows and get stimulated!

I wondered if we'd get clean with the bucket treatment. I emerged from the warm steam squeaky clean with silken hair. We felt great. Things were looking up.

After we left the banya, we could smell our reward: breakfast. We took our turn in line with the other guests and waited to be seated at a big white wooden table with a blue vase filled with wild poppies. We helped ourselves to a steaming plate of hot eggs and potatoes with hot coffee. Life's little pleasures.

We didn't have a honeymoon suite with chilled champagne waiting for us next to a king-size bed made up with luxury linens. No room service or top-of-the-world view. Still, we treasure our memories of the McCarthy bed and breakfast. We had a bed and a banya, a ladder to the John and a tumble in a kamikaze bed!

Fresh Raspberry Topping

This is an old fashioned way to preserve the taste of fresh raspberries. In December we are still spooning this easy concoction over pancakes, waffles, or ice cream. It couldn't be simpler.

Measure the amount of fresh raspberries you have.
Measure the same quantity of sugar.
Using a wooden spoon, mix both in a glass container.
Use a tight-fitting a non-metal lid.
Mix everyday for two weeks.
Serve.

CHAPTER 13

Winter Dance in Healy

I've considered renaming our bed and breakfast "Three Dog Night." Having three dogs clearly puts us over the Alaska average of two and a half per household. Guests know we have a doggy family when they reserve a room. No surprises. The dogs have been to charm school; they have better manners than the average teenager. In fact, guests usually remember the dogs' names before they do mine.

As bed and breakfast co-hosts, the dogs are popular with guests. When one of our pretty female guests asked if Basil, our big springer spaniel, could sleep with her, I had to disappoint her (and probably Basil too). I was quite certain Basil would consider it his duty to jump into bed with all future guests, whether they wanted him or not. There'd be a good chance he was wet at the time. She had to sleep alone.

However well mannered dogs are, they will, when the occasion warrants it, give their opinion. Barking for a dog is a social event. The more dogs, the more intense the conversation. Our dogs announce guests' arrival with "Yippee, yippee, they're here!" After everyone has been properly introduced, things mellow out. Still, there's that awkward moment.

If three dogs can make for a noisy welcome, can you imagine what enthusiasm a dog team could show? Typically, dog mushers live out of town, where the din isn't a problem. A lot full of dogs bark a lot. However, there's a remarkable bed and breakfast-type lodge in Healy where the owners, Jon and Karin, stand in alpha position over an entire team of Alaskan huskies.

Jon has taught his huskies the impossible: to be silent. Well, almost. Once each day, when Jon feeds the team, he lets them have a morning bark. Jon has been guiding guests on sled dog excursions through the Denali wilderness for years.

He and his wife have a sweet love story. Jon's mushing fame reached to the Midwest, where a young woman reading an outdoors magazine read his story and saw his picture. She was feisty enough to send Jon a letter, and it wasn't long before soft-haired Karin came to Alaska to become Jon's wife. I wonder if she had any idea how hard she would work.

I've known people who have paid out their money and youth building a lodge in the wilderness. But once the work is done, they are exhausted and often broke. New owners have to keep the dream going.

But somehow Jon and Karin made it. The lodge rises like a natural cathedral from the high tundra. They have the tallest mountains in North America in their backyard. There are hand-hewn log cabins with interiors brightened by Karin's handicrafts. Jon and Karin must see that guests and employees are fed, housed, and happy and still have enough energy left over to run mushing expeditions. Most amazing to me is that although I know fatigue must be part of their daily routine, they are bright-eyed and enthusiastic.

In winter, most Alaskans try to find a warm beach to fight cabin fever. They look for bargain airfares to Hawaii or Mexico. Not us. We decided to celebrate the long, dark winter with a weekend at Jon and Karin's place. We talked another couple into braving the frigid February temperatures that bottom out in Alaska's Interior. As we drove through the cold night toward Healy, our headlights reflected on the surface of the deep snow cover. Everything—road, fir trees, junk along the highway—it all sparkled at forty degrees below zero.

Once there, we unloaded gear and dogs into our individual cabins. Pronto. Good lord, it was cold. It didn't feel that cold in the dry, still night, but we found out we'd better keep our gloves on. Our fingers tended to flash-freeze to the car doors. It's also unusual to feel your nose hairs freeze up. No toilets in the cabins. Too cold for them to function. There'd be some quick night sprints to the lodge bathhouse.

The next morning broke clear and cold. We could see the sun's reluctant rising from the high hills that surrounded us. At breakfast we met the lodge's other guests, a Frenchman and his adult son. They had spent the previous day with Jon preparing for a one-week mushing expedition in Denali National Park. They would each be riding their own sled, loaded with supplies and pulled by a full team of dogs. They had learned to pack the sled and to harness and handle their own team. They would be staying in cabins at night, but both men were so thin that I wondered about their ability to stay warm.

The next morning, Karin, my friend Tess, and I went out to see the teams off. Jon and the guests were loading the sleds, checking gear as they went. The French guests certainly looked warm enough in heavy Arctic clothing.

We women bundled together in the cold light. Our husbands had already gone ptarmigan hunting.

Watching the preparations, Karin spoke admiringly of her husband: "When Jon is on the back of that sled, he's a dancer." And handsome too, I thought.

Finally, they were ready to leave. The noise had become deafening. Not only were the dogs in harness barking, but the dogs still tied next to their doghouses had an opinion too. Jon was the first out with his team in the lead, shouting, "Hike, hike, hike." The sleds with the Frenchman and his son followed. There were sound and fury as the dogs hit their harnesses. Those dogs wanted to run.

We watched the teams as, one by one, they climbed the hills, through the spruce and out again to a higher plateau toward the lower reaches of Denali National Park. As men and dogs wound through the final visible stands of trees, it became very quiet. I felt like one of the dogs in the lot. Left behind.

Tess walked slowly through the scrub, following the sled trail through the spruce until we lost sight of her. I knew she would be back soon; she was walking in the direction of her heart. I was a little wistful myself. Maybe I too longed to be hardier, younger, and quick enough to dance behind a team of rowdy huskies.

* * *

It was a Saturday night in Healy. There'd be a dance that night at the school gym. Music to be provided by a popular Athabascan fiddler. Everyone was going. While Tess and I were excited, our husbands were less enthusiastic. Healy has about a thousand people, twice the number of men as women. We needed escorts.

This brings us to one of the differences between men and women. Very scientific, of course. It's about dancing.

Women love to dance. Adult men, on the other hand, are like male birds. When around females, they puff up, look good, and have cool moves. Dancing is courtship behavior. But when the dust settles on the nest, they'd rather sit it out. Those are the facts.

Considering the Venus-Mars conflict here, how noble it was that our husbands helped us get parka'd up to our eyebrows against the minus-zero cold for a romp in the gym.

It was a cheerful scene at Healy High School. Free hot dogs and soft drinks, beer for sale, and everyone got a plastic gift mug that said "First Annual Healy Winter Festival." The place was full of locals, mostly men and children running amok. The gym smelled like warm wool and fur. The fiddler had just finishing his tuning when he launched the evening with "Tennessee Waltz."

As we sat there feeling like the strangers in town that we were, I was reminded of a grange farmer's dance I went to when I was a little girl. My daddy asked me to dance. I stood on the top of his shoes as he waltzed sedately around the room with me holding his legs tightly. I was so proud to be a daddy's girl. At midnight, there had been a pancake breakfast. Can you imagine anything more magical to a child than to dance, run around with other kids, stay up late, and finally eat a big breakfast in the middle of the night?

I bobbed my head to the wonderful rhythmic dips in the fiddler's version of "Tennessee Waltz." I looked over at Tess. She too was dancing in her chair. We watched the couples on the floor, just a few brave souls. Tess and I exchanged glances and then looked over longingly at our husbands, who were happy to chat and drink beer.

Finally, I couldn't stand it anymore. I felt like a seventh-grader in junior high, when the boys would stand on one side of the gym talking to their buddies and looking goofy while the girls would stand on the other side just dying to be asked to dance.

It was time to stop the madness. I leaned over and whispered to my husband, "Please, honey, just one slow one." My husband, like the good man he is, held out his hand. Tess's husband followed his lead. The four of us stumbled around the best we could for a few minutes before we sat down, relieved that it was over. My toes had been stepped on pretty good, but not by me. I realized that where there is a will, there isn't necessarily rhythm.

Someone must have made a move to leave, because even though it was early in the evening, we all seemed to be pulling on our coats to leave. I had just zipped up my heavy parka when the fiddler launched into a spirited "Turkey in the Straw." Tess looked over at me and asked, "Would you like to dance?"

"You bet," I replied.

Then we were on the floor with Tess leading. I don't know if the fiddler sped up or we did, but the men's amazed faces blurred as we whirled faster and faster. I thought I was going to have heat stroke as we whirled like beer-besotted dervishes around the floor. When the music stopped, we were red faced from dancing in our parkas. Although our husbands looked a bit befuddled, I was glad Tess had asked me to dance. That Midwestern farm girl knew how to polka!

Northern lights were flashing in the clear, starry night when we got back to our cabins. Without city lights to obscure the glow of the aurora, we could see the reds, greens, and blues as bright as a photo in a coffee table book. But a picture could never capture the flash dance of the aurora's ribbons of light, folding and arching, flooding the entire sky with disco brilliance. Maybe everyone becomes a believer under a northern sky. God has his night moves down real good.

We silently watched the lights, necks twisted upward. I've heard that the lights don't really crackle, but when you talk out loud, it does seem like you're interrupting some cosmic conversation. I was having deep thoughts, but my fingers were starting to turn numb when someone finally yelled "Uncle!" and we broke for the warmth of our cabins and each other's arms.

Romantic Japanese believe that a child conceived under the aurora is blessed. That charming tradition brings many visitors from Japan to Alaska's Interior during the winter months. Of course the display is good for winter travel business, but we tend to snicker when we talk about love, lust, and the northern lights.

Still, everyone has the right to be wrong. Nine months after we had celebrated winter with our friends, Tess gave birth to a daughter. The couple named her Aurora.

CHAPTER 14

Why You Wouldn't Do It for the Money

A dinner invitation from a casual acquaintance often means my new friend wants to start a bed and breakfast. I've just taken my first sip of wine when the first question comes.

"So how do you like running a bed and breakfast?"

My hosts have an extra bedroom and a spare set of sheets, and, by golly, it sounds like fun.

I've seriously thought of a handing out a business card that says "B&B consulting: First five minutes FREE." But of course I don't, because I'm too nice for that. I politely answer their questions:

"Do you like running a bed and breakfast?"

Of course I enjoy running the bed and breakfast. I'm no masochist. Bed and breakfast people are different, fun, and more independent. And every person has a story. Some guests volunteer to tell you theirs; with others you guess and glimpse. I meet people who take my heart as they leave.

Occasionally guests send us embarrassingly generous thank-you gifts. One guest sent a crystal vase from her recently deceased mother's estate. She said that when she saw it, she thought of my garden. People usually give more than they take. I want to tell you about just one.

Last summer, we hosted a beautiful biologist from India named Nann. She was researching the spruce bark beetle that has devastated Alaska's forests. She wore large aquamarine earrings given to her by her jeweler father, and precious as they were, what she held in her hands was more so.

She had borrowed some old journals written by a biologist in the 1940s. They contained his observations of the spruce bark beetle, which was a destructive little devil even then. We turned the brittle pages carefully as we read his entries. I think because the journal was handwritten, we felt the author's presence more acutely. At one point, the biologist's writing started to wander downward off the page.

He explained in his elegant script, "The airplane I'm in is rolling so hard in this storm, even the ink doesn't know which way is up!" Naan and I marveled that he could be tossed about in a storm and still make a joke. The two of us spent the evening in the fine company of a man long gone.

"Do you ever get a 'bad' guest?"

We could count on one hand, over twenty years, the number of times we were glad to see people go. Guests are on their good behavior in our home. Often we host visiting grandparents. We really have a chance to enjoy them, and they get to sleep at night in a quiet, kiddie-free home. I remind guests: "Come home for an afternoon nap. You're on vacation!"

When there is a problem, I try to figure it out. I see it as a challenge. Recently, a hotel referred a guest to us. I suspect it was trying to get rid of her. She was a tense executive who was used to supervising a raft of employees. When she wasn't on her cell phone barking instructions to her staff, she was supervising me.

She evaluated everything, from breakfast to bed, in detail. Why she liked something if she did, why she didn't like it if she didn't. The queen must be pleased.

"You don't have an ironing board with an iron in my room. Oh well, I keep forgetting, this isn't a hotel." She just couldn't stop micromanaging.

One afternoon, she popped in while I was mopping the hardwood floor and observed: "I see there are wet spots on the floor. Is that from the puppy?"

What?! She's supervising my housekeeping? I rounded on her with my teacher's "just about –to –go ballistic" look.

"Don't you have something to do today other than keep an eye on me?" My guest did a one-eighty. She'd been shoving and I finally shoved back. Nothing else was said about the incident, but she was a lamb after that. Very sweet.

Our temperamental guest sent us a box of jams from Oregon to thank us. It works both ways, though. If she ever returns, she'll find an ironing board and an iron in her room.

"Do you have to get up in the morning?"

I hate getting up early.

The Anchorage international airport wakes up around 10:00 p.m. You can tell who lives here and who doesn't. The townies look crummy but perky. Visitors look well dressed, stressed, and dead tired. It's been a long day to get from Wherever, Lower 48, to this, the last stop. By the time a guest gets the baggage and a cab or rental car, it's midnight or later. Even that wouldn't be so bad, but bus and train tours typically leave before eight in the morning. It makes for a brief night.

Short answer. You can do one or the other. Run a bed and breakfast or sleep. Not both.

Is it necessary to fix a big breakfast? I was thinking I'd just serve muffins, coffee, and juice. Most people don't want all that food anyway.

In the evening, I always ask guests if they'd like a light breakfast, maybe cereal and fruit, or a full breakfast. Almost everyone opts for the whole enchilada.

Breakfast is, as far as I'm concerned, part of the experience. I like to present guests with a plate of fresh fruit or a fruit parfait. Gourmet coffee served with real cream and sugar in an antique bowl. A full breakfast entree such as wild salmon omelets with herbs or baked French toast with Alaska blueberries and cream I've whipped myself. Juice and pastries. I put out my nicest things with fresh flowers and cloth napkins. It's expensive to serve and takes time to prepare, but it's worth it. Food is love.

So, I'm thinking about using the downstairs with the private entrance. I was thinking that we could put in a little refrigerator and a microwave. We really wouldn't see the guests that much. We'd still have our privacy.

If guests wanted privacy, they'd stay in a hotel. They want to talk to you. They have questions: where to eat, go, shop. How, when, and why did you come to Alaska? Do you get moose? How much snow is there in winter? Where can I buy a toothbrush? When does your husband get home so I can ask him some questions about _____? I find guests will knock on my closed bedroom door, just to chat.

Forget privacy. Hospitality is the only real reason you would invite strangers in, day after day, to share your home and life. The loss of privacy is so complete that you couldn't possibly do it just for the money.

There is a formula that works for me: My personal enjoyment equals the amount of time I'm able to give my guests. Time is my gift to them.

"Is hosting a bed and breakfast a lot of work?"

Are you serious? You mean fixing and serving breakfast, conversing with guests, cleaning bedrooms and bathrooms, making beds, doing the laundry, grocery shopping, keeping up the house and garden as well as getting ready to meet today's arrivals?

Last winter, a group of young women athletes spent a week with us. After their departure, I had to replace a curtain rod and a shade, clean a sofa, and unstop a toilet. I have my own toolbox.

Recently, a family group stayed with us to attend their son's wedding. Their daughter and her friend became wretchedly sick with the flu. Because the rest of the family was doing the wedding thing, the kids needed TLC. I took care of them.

After my guests left, I had to strip the room to the walls, duvets, featherbeds, linen, pillows. Everything had to be washed, cleaned, and, in some cases, replaced. There are inconveniences that just come with doing business.

Some potential owners hope to make running a bed and breakfast a family endeavor.

Bad idea. Would your children be good little helpers? One bed and breakfast brochure promises that their two children would be happy to play a piano and violin duet for you, if you ask them. Not to be cynical, but isn't that why most people go on vacation?

A host could hire some cheap labor to help. It hasn't worked for me. In a small bed and breakfast, the cost of an employee just eats up the profits. Neighborhood kids will work for less money, but they're unreliable.

It can be helpful if there are two of you to share the work. But a spouse hardly wants to play host/handyman when he/she comes home from another job. In fact, often one partner works just to pay for the frequent additions to the property. Owners can't resist making the nest bigger and fancier.

Trust me. You're going to work all the time, because your work is always with you in your own home. It's going to be hard to find good help. In fact, I'll bet my apron that at the end of the day you'll still be the maid.

My dinner host is looking more thoughtful. My reality check has played havoc with an "I don't want to feed 'em or see 'em" mentality. The mentality that says, "Just show me the money."

When I was a new teacher, a good friend advised me: "Get a three-by-five card and write down why you come to work. Then put that card where you'll be able to see it every day."

I still have the card. Its message works for life in general and equally well for running a bed and breakfast. The card says:

"Do it because you love them."

Order info:

www.sherrytomlinson.alaskawriters.com

PARISH LITURGIES
EXPERIMENTS AND RESOURCES
IN SUNDAY WORSHIP